Philip Kerr, Sue Kay & Vaug

Inside Out

Workbook

MACMILLAN

Macmillan Education
Between Towns Road, Oxford OX4 3PP, UK
A division of Macmillan Publishers Limited
Companies and representatives throughout the world

ISBN 0 333 97588X (International Edition)
ISBN 0 333 99907X (level II)

Text © Philip Kerr, Sue Kay and Vaughan Jones
Design and illustration © Macmillan Publishers Limited 2002

First published 2002

Project management by Desmond O'Sullivan, ELT Publishing Services
Edited by Alyson Maskell, Phoenix Publishing Services
Designed by Jackie Hill at 320 Design
Illustrated by Martin Chatterton pp 12, 22, 51, 62, 65, 81; Mark Thomas
pp15, 75; Ed McLachlan pp17, 29, 47, 64, 69, 77; Julian Mosedale pp21,
37, 79; Shelagh McNicholas pp26, 43, 46, 83.
Cover design by Andrew Oliver
Cover painting *After Visiting David Hockney* © Howard Hodgkin

The authors and publishers would like to thank the following for
permission to reproduce copyright material:

Extracts on pp19, 68 from *The Mammoth Book of Jokes* edited by Geoff
Tibballs (Robinson, 2000), reprinted by permission of Constable &
Robinson Publishing Ltd; extract on p72 (bottom right) from *Collins Gem
Book: Ghosts* by Karen Hurrell and Janet Bord (HarperCollins, 2000),
reprinted by permission of HarperCollins Publishers Ltd; extract on p73
from *The Unexplained Strange People* by Jamie Stokes (Parragon, 2000),
reprinted by permission of the publisher.

The authors and publishers would like to thank the following for
permission to reproduce their photographs:

Corbis p76(t, b), Corbis / Christopher Cox p33, Corbis / James Davis
p9(b), Corbis / David Lees p55, Corbis / Karen Huntt-Mason p9(m),
Corbis / Mona Lisa (1503–1505) Leonardo da Vinci: Gianni Dagli Orti
p45, Corbis / Matthew Polak p25, Corbis / Vine Streano p7(m), Corbis /
Patrick Ward p9(t), Corbis – Sygma / Sunset Boulevard p48; FPG p71
(goldfish); Hulton Archive pp13, 73; Image Bank pp71 (dog, hamster);
Stone pp11, 71(t, cat), 76(b); Telegraph Colour Library p7(t).

Printed and bound in Spain by Edelvives

2006 2005 2004 2003
10 9 8 7 6 5 4 3

Level II
10 9 8 7 6 5 4 3 2 1

get 1
get 2 } 1/2
go 3 4

Free 1
Free 2
Free 3
Free 4

1 Me

Grammar

1 Complete the questions with an appropriate question word. Then circle the correct answer.

Example
<u>Who</u> was married to the actor Bruce Willis?

a) Cher b) Cristina Aguilera (c) Demi Moore)

1 _____ is the actor Nicholas Cage's real surname?
   a) Coppola b) Lucas c) Spielberg

2 _____ Beatle was really called Richard Starkey?
   a) John Lennon b) Paul McCartney
   c) Ringo Starr

3 _____ does Elton John come from?
   a) Edinburgh b) London c) New York

4 _____ was the film *Titanic* made?
   a) 1997 b) 1998 c) 1999

2 The conversation below is with a web robot (similar to A.L.I.C.E.) called John Lennon. Circle the correct verb form.

A: (Do you miss)/ *Miss you* Yoko?
B: Yoko's always in my thoughts.
A: (a) *Argued you / Did you argue* with Paul?
B: No, I didn't argue with Paul. (b) *Is that / That is* important?
A: (c) *Do like you / Do you like* the music of Oasis?
B: I don't know if I like the music of Oasis. I love TV shows about the Rolling Stones.
A: What (d) *is your favourite Beatles song? / your favourite Beatles song is?*
B: 'Here, There and Everywhere' ... just beautiful.
A: (e) *Do you think / Think you* the world is becoming more peaceful?
B: I don't think about it.

3 Insert an auxiliary verb (*do, does, did*) in the questions below **where necessary**. Some of the questions do not need an auxiliary.

Example
    did
Where ⁄you learn English?

a) How much you weigh?

b) Who speaks the best English in your class?

c) How often your teacher give you homework?

d) What you have for breakfast today?

e) Which languages can you speak?

f) Which party won the last election?

4 Rearrange the words to make questions.

Example
name original Elton John's was What ?
What was Elton John's original name?

a) change David Bowie's did his name son why ?
QUASI   QASI
<u>Why did David Bowie's son change his name?</u>

b) London his after Who part named of daughter a ?
<u>Who named his daughter after a part of London?</u>

c) A.L.I.C.E. does How languages many speak ?
QASI
<u>How many languages does A.L.C.E speak?</u>

d) did John Lennon record *Stand By Me* When ?
<u>When did John Lennon record Stand By Me?</u>

Now answer the questions. The answers are all in Unit 1 of your coursebook.

Example
<u>Reginald Kenneth Dwight</u>

a) _____

b) _____

c) _____

d) _____

Reading

1 Read the stories below and match each story to a title.

- **How stupid can you be?**
- **The world's most inappropriate name**
- **Will you marry me?**

a

One day, a man lost his dog. (1) He put an advertisement in the newspaper and hoped that somebody would telephone him with news of his pet. It was easy to identify the dog. It had only three legs and had also lost an ear in a fight with a rotweiler. Unfortunately, the dog was blind, too – the result of a fight with a cat. (2) And if someone found the dog, they could check its name. It had a tag around its neck with its name on it: 'Lucky'!

b

The British conductor Sir Thomas Beecham was walking one day with a friend of his sister's. (3) Her name was Utica Wells. Beecham turned to the girl and said, 'I don't like your first name. I'd like to change it.' 'You can't do that,' she replied, 'but you can change my surname.' (4) They got married soon afterwards.

c

A woman, Mrs Smith, was in hospital after the birth of her son. (5) She was trying to decide what to call her son, when she walked past a door. It had the name 'KING' on it. That's a good name, she thought. A little later, she walked past another door, and this time she saw the name 'NOSMO'. (6) But she liked it, too, and so her son was named Nosmo King Smith. It was only six months later that she discovered her terrible mistake.

2 Where do these missing sentences belong in the stories opposite? Write the number in the box.

a) He looked at her and smiled. ☐

b) He was afraid that something terrible had happened. ☐ 1

c) It had no hair on its bottom – after an accident with an electric fire. ☐

d) It was their first date. ☐

e) Strange, but interesting, she thought. ☐

f) When she was feeling well again, she went for a walk. ☐

3 Read the stories again and write questions for the following answers.

Example
Where *did the man put an advertisement?*

In the newspaper. (*story a*)

a) How many _____

_____ ?

Three. (*story a*)

b) What _____

_____ ?

A name tag. (*story a*)

c) What _____

_____ ?

He was a conductor. (*story b*)

d) Which _____

_____ ?

Her first name. (*story b*)

e) When _____

_____ ?

Soon afterwards. (*story b*)

f) Where _____

_____ ?

On a door. (*story c*)

g) When _____

_____ ?

Six months later. (*story c*)

Vocabulary

1 Read the information and complete the names on John Lennon's family tree.

- Julian's step-mother is called Yoko.
- Julian's half-brother has a partner called Yuka.
- One of John Lennon's half-sisters had the same name as his mother.
- Mimi has a niece called Jacqui.
- Sean had a great-grandmother called Mary.

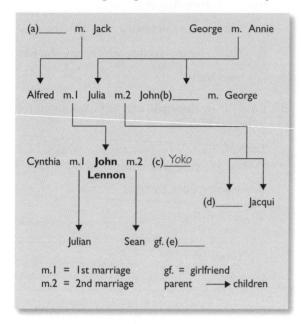

(a)_____ m. Jack   George m. Annie

Alfred m.1 Julia m.2 John(b)_____ m. George

Cynthia m.1 **John** m.2 (c) _Yoko_
          Lennon

(d)_____ Jacqui

Julian   Sean gf. (e)_____

m.1 = 1st marriage   gf. = girlfriend
m.2 = 2nd marriage   parent ──▶ children

2 Look at the completed family tree and say if the following sentences are true (T) or false (F).

a) John Lennon was Mimi's nephew. ☐

b) Alfred's ex-wife was called Julia. ☐

c) Yoko was Jack's daughter-in-law. ☐

d) Annie was Cynthia's aunt. ☐

e) Julian was Jacqui's stepson. ☐

f) Annie didn't have any great-grandchildren. ☐

g) George's father-in-law was also called George. ☐

h) John Lennon had an uncle called Jack. ☐

3 In the following sentences, delete *like* when it should not be there. Four sentences are correct.

Example
He always looks ~~like~~ terrible early in the morning.

a) He sounds like a very friendly person.

b) My ex-husband looked like a macho cowboy.

c) They looked like a bit tired after the lesson.

d) She looks like a typical, middle-aged mum.

e) She sounds like foreign – is she Greek?

f) My father-in-law looks like Dracula. Only joking!

g) You look like stressed out. What's up?

4 Match the sentence beginnings in box A with their endings in box B.

A

a) I think he has nothing
b) In the 1950s, many parents called
c) In the next few days, I need to make
d) Madonna recorded
e) Many people believe
f) She didn't pay
g) The exercise is very easy if you follow
h) They want their children to grow

B

1 a decision about my future.
2 attention, so she didn't understand.
3 her first song in 1982.
4 in common with his girlfriend.
5 up in a safe, quiet place.
6 the simple instructions.
7 their children Susan or Peter.
8 in life after death.

5 Complete each sentence with a word from the box.

au pair   banker   doctor
police officer   psychologist   student
used-car salesman   waiter

a) A _____ buys and sells old motor vehicles.

b) A _____ helps people who are ill.

c) A _____ investigates crimes.

d) A _____ has an important position in a bank.

e) A _____ serves food in a restaurant.

f) A _____ studies the human mind.

g) A _____ goes to school, college or university.

h) An _____ looks after other people's children and does housework.

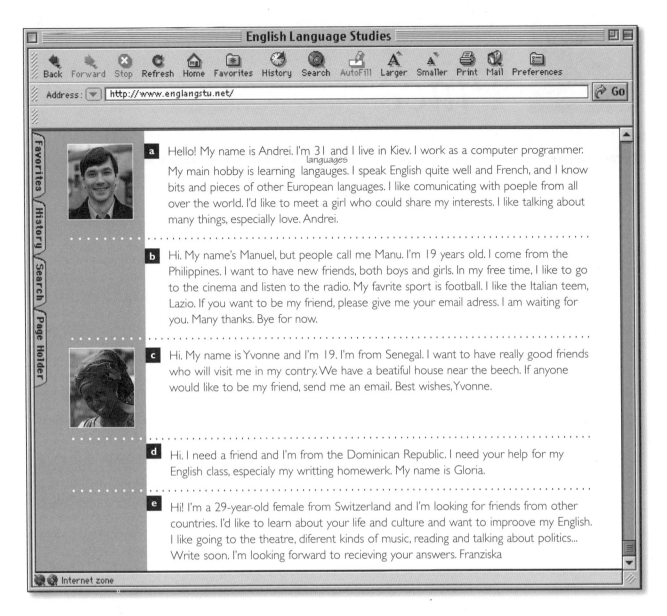

The content of the browser window:

English Language Studies

Address: http://www.englangstu.net/

a Hello! My name is Andrei. I'm 31 and I live in Kiev. I work as a computer programmer.
My main hobby is learning ~~langauges~~ *languages*. I speak English quite well and French, and I know bits and pieces of other European languages. I like comunicating with poeple from all over the world. I'd like to meet a girl who could share my interests. I like talking about many things, especially love. Andrei.

b Hi. My name's Manuel, but people call me Manu. I'm 19 years old. I come from the Philippines. I want to have new friends, both boys and girls. In my free time, I like to go to the cinema and listen to the radio. My favrite sport is football. I like the Italian teem, Lazio. If you want to be my friend, please give me your email adress. I am waiting for you. Many thanks. Bye for now.

c Hi. My name is Yvonne and I'm 19. I'm from Senegal. I want to have really good friends who will visit me in my contry. We have a beatiful house near the beech. If anyone would like to be my friend, send me an email. Best wishes, Yvonne.

d Hi. I need a friend and I'm from the Dominican Republic. I need your help for my English class, especialy my writting homewerk. My name is Gloria.

e Hi! I'm a 29-year-old female from Switzerland and I'm looking for friends from other countries. I'd like to learn about your life and culture and want to improove my English. I like going to the theatre, diferent kinds of music, reading and talking about politics... Write soon. I'm looking forward to recieving your answers. Franziska

Internet zone

Writing

1 The messages above were posted on a website for English language students. Each message has three spelling mistakes. Find the mistakes and correct them.

2 Choose one message and write a short reply (50–80 words).

Pronunciation

1 Match the words in each column which have the same vowel sounds.

aunt	call	daughter
mean	improve	feel
movie	father	girl
sport	learn	grew
surname	niece	partner

🎧 Listen to the recording to check your answers.

2 What are the words below?

Example

/miː/   *me* _____

a) /pɑːt/ _____
b) /wiːl/ _____
c) /tuːl/ _____
d) /fɜːst/ _____
e) /bɔːn/ _____

🎧 Listen to the recording to check your answers.

2 Place

Grammar

1 Write the plurals of the nouns in the correct column.

> ~~beach~~   brush   ~~child~~   church   ~~city~~
> ~~holiday~~   man   quality   statue
> summary   taxi   tooth   tourist
> university   watch   woman

Plurals ending in 's'
holidays
_____
_____
_____

Plurals ending in 'ies'
cities
_____
_____
_____

Plurals ending in 'es'
beaches
_____
_____
_____

Irregular plurals
children
_____
_____
_____

2 Each sentence contains *one* mistake. Correct the mistakes.

Example

I'd like some advices about restaurants in the city, please.

a) You need to make more progresses with your mathematics!

b) Two customs officers wanted to look at my luggages.

c) The students in the class had a lot of homeworks.

d) There was a lot of informations on the TV news about the elections in Canada and Ireland.

e) I haven't got enough moneys to go to restaurants every day.

f) They bought some breads to make sandwiches.

g) Many Americans enjoy the fresh airs and spectacular views of the Rocky Mountains.

3 Complete the questions with *much* or *many*.

Example

How <u>many</u> books did you read last year?

a) How _____ bread do you eat every day?

b) How _____ homework does your teacher give you?

c) How _____ money do you have with you now?

d) How _____ people in your town are unemployed?

e) How _____ progress do you think you will make with your English this year?

f) How _____ restaurants have you been to in your town?

g) How _____ students are there in your school?

Now answer the questions. Use a word or phrase from the box.

> a few   a little   a lot   lots   none
> not many   not much   one

4 Complete the sentences about London with *much, many, a little* or *a few*.

a) How _____ do you know about London?

b) London only gets _____ snow in the winter.

c) Not _____ people in restaurants speak languages other than English.

d) Only _____ policemen have guns.

e) The Queen stays at Buckingham Palace only _____ times each year.

f) There are too _____ castles to visit in one day.

g) There is not _____ modern architecture.

h) You do not see _____ traffic in the city centre.

Now decide if sentences b) – h) are true (T) or false (F).

Listening

1 📼 Cover the tapescript opposite and listen to the recording. Which place is the speaker describing?

2 📼 Listen again and decide if the following sentences are true (T) or false (F).

a) He first went to Marrakech four or five years ago. ☐

b) He went there for his summer holidays. ☐

c) He travelled with his girlfriend. ☐

d) He stayed with the family of a friend. ☐

e) After dinner, he visited the Koutoubia Mosque. ☐

f) Djemaa el Fna is the name of his favourite café. ☐

g) There is a lot to see in the main square. ☐

h) You can see the Atlas Mountains from the city. ☐

i) He has been there six times. ☐

j) His last visit was three months ago. ☐

Correct the sentences that are false.

I suppose the most interesting, and the most exciting, place I've ever been is Marrakech. I first went there many years ago, maybe ten, twelve years, I can't remember exactly. I was living and working in Casablanca, which is, oh, I don't know, about four or five hours from Marrakech. We had a long weekend, and Dave and I – he was my best friend at the time, we both had the same name and people called us the two Daves – we were looking for something to do. There was a guy we worked with, Malik, and he invited us to come and stay with his family.

So we all set off on a Thursday evening after work, and eventually we got to Marrakech. His family live in an amazing house very near to the main square, the Djemaa el Fna. His mum cooked us dinner and then we all went to the market square. We sat on the roof terrace of a café, drinking mint tea, and watching the action in the square below. It really is the most incredible place in the world. There are people buying and selling absolutely everything. There are loads of little 'kitchens', serving soup and kebabs and snails and everything. You can listen to story-tellers (if you speak Arabic, that is), watch snake charmers, acrobats, jugglers. On the Saturday, I even saw a group of men on camels! Their faces were painted blue and they had come from the desert in the south of the country.

There are loads of other things to see and do. The Koutoubia Mosque is spectacular and all the tourists go there. The views are out of this world, with the Atlas Mountains in the distance, and there are some beautiful parks, like the garden that belonged to Yves St Laurent. It's got great restaurants. Everything about it is great.

But it's the square, the Djemaa el Fna, and the shopping streets around it, that make Marrakech really special. Every time I go back to Marrakech, and I've probably been there ten or twelve times, I go straight to the square and sit on my favourite café terrace. If I ever have the money, I'd love to buy a house there. But for the moment, it's just a dream. Right now, I don't even have a job and the last time I went was three years ago. Hey, would you like to see my photos?

Vocabulary

1 Complete each sentence with a word from the box.

> beach castle church fountain hill
> office block square statue

a) Have you seen the _____ of Shakespeare outside the theatre?

b) Let's go swimming at the _____ .

c) On Saturdays, there is a market in the large _____ in the middle of the town.

d) She works in a new _____ in the business area of the town.

e) The _____ was built in the sixteenth century to defend the city.

f) The park is on a _____ and has good views of the city.

g) They wanted to have a traditional wedding in a _____ .

h) Throw some money into the _____ : it will bring you good luck.

2 Search the word square (↑ ↓ → ←) for fifteen adjectives. Eight adjectives can be used to describe things you like and seven adjectives can be used to describe things you do not like.

S	U	S	E	L	E	S	S	C	Q
P	D	U	L	L	S	G	G	I	M
E	E	Y	L	G	U	N	N	T	I
C	L	J	G	G	O	I	I	S	S
T	B	L	R	N	L	T	T	A	E
A	I	U	E	I	U	I	S	T	R
C	R	F	A	Z	B	C	U	N	A
U	R	W	T	A	A	X	G	A	B
L	E	A	X	M	F	E	S	F	L
A	T	T	R	A	C	T	I	V	E
R	Y	L	E	V	O	L	D	Z	O

things you like
spectacular
amazing
lovely
_____
_____
_____
_____

things you don't like
ugly
_____
_____
_____
_____
_____

3 Complete each sentence with a country adjective.

Example
A sombrero is a Mexican hat.

a) Bordeaux is a F_____ wine.

b) Fuji is a J_____ mountain.

c) Goulash is a H_____ dish.

d) Guinness is an I_____ beer.

e) Inter Milan is an I_____ football team.

f) Lisbon is the P_____ capital.

g) The Great Pyramid is an E_____ monument.

h) The tango is an A_____ dance.

4 Complete the sentences with *in, on* or *at.*

Example
The restaurants are great; in fact, they're the best in the world.

a) I sometimes wish all the tourists would leave us _____ peace.

b) Many tourists come to the city to take part _____ the Mardi Gras carnival.

c) Sitges is a town _____ the coast, not far from Barcelona.

d) The best residential areas are _____ the north and west of the city.

e) The parks are all _____ the other side of town.

f) The place is dead during the day, but it comes alive _____ night.

g) There are four prizes _____ offer in the fantastic competition.

Pronunciation

Look at the box of verbs from this unit that have two syllables. Do they have the stress on the first or the second syllable? Put them into the correct column.

> ~~decide~~ describe discuss ~~enter~~ explain
> happen label listen mention practise
> relax repeat suppose visit

Oo	oO
enter	decide
_____	_____
_____	_____
_____	_____
_____	_____
_____	_____

Listen to the recording to check your answers.

Writing

1 Replace the underlined words and phrases in the postcard with a word or phrase from the list.

a few days ago	go in the afternoon	Mum and Dad	some interesting ruins
evening	Helsinki	places of interest	take photographs
fabulous	lots	professor of archaeology	terrible
food	Love	sightseeing	

Dear <u>Bill</u>,

I got here <u>last Friday</u> and I'm having a <u>great</u> time. The weather is <u>not good</u>, but there are <u>plenty</u> of things to do. There are a few <u>cafés</u> near the hotel where I <u>play cards</u> and <u>chat with other tourists</u>. I've met a <u>lovely girl</u> from <u>Madrid</u> who is taking me to a <u>great new club</u> tomorrow. The <u>nightlife</u> is interesting – so different from at home. I'm always really tired in the <u>morning</u> after so much <u>going out</u> – I'll need a holiday after this!

<u>Best wishes</u>

Simon

2 Now write your own postcard. Replace the underlined words with words of your own choice.

3 Couples

Grammar

1 Put the verbs in brackets into the past simple.

Romeo <u>was</u> (be) in love with Rosaline but one day at a party he (a) _____ (meet) Juliet. He immediately (b) _____ (fall) in love with her and (c) _____ (forget) all about Rosaline. Unfortunately, Romeo's family (d) _____ (be) enemies of Juliet's family. Her family (e) _____ (want) her to marry someone else. To cut a long story short, Romeo (f) _____ (kill) himself because he (g) _____ (think) that Juliet (h) _____ (be) dead. Then, Juliet (i) _____ (wake) up and (j) _____ (find) Romeo's body. So she (k) _____ (take) Romeo's sword and (l) _____ (kill) herself, too.

2 Read the text in exercise 1 again and write questions for the following answers.

Example
Who <u>was Romeo in love</u> with?
Rosaline.

a) Where _____ ?
At a party.

b) Who _____ about?
Rosaline.

c) Who _____ marry?
Someone else.

d) Who _____ ?
Himself.

e) Why _____ ?
Because he thought Juliet was dead.

f) What _____
when she woke up?
She killed herself, too.

g) How _____ ?
With Romeo's sword.

3 Look at the picture of a modern Romeo and Juliet. Complete each sentence with a verb from the box in the past continuous.

feel   get   hold   hope   make   sit
speak   ~~wear~~

Example
Juliet <u>was wearing</u> an old T-shirt.

a) She _____ a cup of coffee.

b) It was late and she _____ tired.

c) Romeo _____ on his motorcyle.

d) He _____ for a date.

e) They _____ on their mobiles.

f) A dog _____ a lot of noise.

g) Romeo _____ wet.

4 Put the verbs in brackets into the correct form. Use the past simple or the past continuous.

Juliet <u>was going</u> (go) out with a man called Paris, but she didn't love him. One evening, she (a) _____ (watch) TV when the telephone rang. It was Romeo and he (b) _____ (say) that he was in the street below. She (c) _____ (open) the door of the balcony and saw him in the street. He (d) _____ (sit) on a motorcycle. When he saw her, he (e) _____ (begin) to sing. It was a beautiful song and Juliet (f) _____ (want) it to last forever. But it (g) _____ (rain) and she was cold and wet. She (h) _____ (decide) to ask Romeo inside. Then, another motorcycle (i) _____ (arrive). It was Paris …

Reading

1 Read the story about the famous opera singer, Maria Callas, and put the paragraphs in the correct order.

1 [B]   2 [ ]   3 [ ]   4 [ ]

2 Put the events below in the correct order.

a) He bought presents for her.
b) He died.
c) He rang her up.
d) Maria got married.
e) Onassis got married.
f) She died.
g) She fell in love.
h) She met Onassis.
i) She split up from her husband.
j) They had rows.
k) They went on holiday together.
l) He asked her to go out with him.

1	2	3	4	5	6	7	8	9	10	11	12
d											f

3 Answer the questions.

a) What happened when Maria was staying in Venice?

_____

_____

b) Why did Maria love Onassis?

_____

_____

c) Why did she have rows with Onassis?

_____

_____

d) How did she find out about Onassis's marriage?

_____

_____

e) Why did Onassis begin visiting Maria again?

_____

_____

f) What was Maria doing on Skorpios?

_____

_____

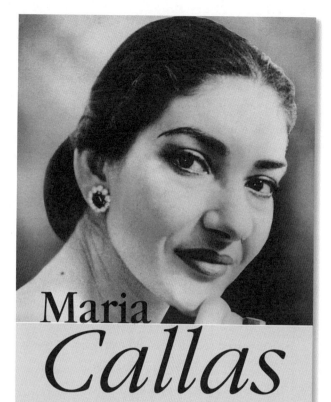

Maria Callas

A At the time, Maria said, 'I have lost everything.' After this, she stayed at home and she did not look after herself. Two years later people could still see her on the island of Skorpios, crying next to the grave of Onassis. A little later, Maria died of a heart attack.

B Maria Callas was singing in Verona when she met the impresario, Giovanni Meneghini. He became her manager and they got married. But Maria was unhappy in the marriage and in 1957, when she was staying in Venice, she met the Greek tycoon, Aristotle Onassis. Onassis began telephoning her. He invited her to parties and he bought her beautiful presents. Maria fell in love with him and, two years later, she and her husband split up.

C She saw him less and less often and then one day in 1968 she was reading the newspaper when she saw a report about his marriage to Jackie Kennedy. It was not a happy marriage and Onassis began to visit Maria again. Sometimes, she agreed to see him; sometimes, she refused. Life continued in this way for some time, but, finally, in 1975, Onassis died.

D Onassis took her on holiday and Maria told reporters that she was in love. She said that she didn't love him for his money but because he was 'the first man to treat me like a woman'. She dreamed of marriage and wanted to have children, but after a while Onassis became tired of the relationship. He was now seeing other women and they had rows.

Vocabulary

1 Put the lines of this love story about Frank Sinatra and Ava Gardner in the right order.

a) When Sinatra fell in

b) relationship, and when they split up, he was

c) love with Ava Gardner he was already

d) only three years, but Ava Gardner was the love

e) married, but he couldn't resist her. He got

f) in love with her.

g) heartbroken. Their marriage lasted

h) of Frank Sinatra's life. Later, Sinatra admitted that he would always be

i) divorced so that he could marry her. It was a stormy

1	2	3	4	5	6	7	8	9
a								f

🔊 Listen to the recording to check your answers.

2 Complete the text with words from the box.

> affair   divorced   dream   lover
> marriage   rumours   unfaithful
> ~~wedding~~

In 1981, Charles, Prince of Wales, married Lady Diana Spencer. The _wedding_ was watched by millions on TV. For the British public, it was a
(a) _____ come true. But for Charles and Diana, it was never a happy
(b) _____ . Charles was
(c) _____ from the start with his
(d) _____ , Camilla Parker Bowles.
After a few years, there began to be
(e) _____ about Diana, too. She had an
(f) _____ with her riding teacher.
Nobody was surprised when Charles and Diana finally got (g) _____ .

3 Complete the sentences with *have* or *get*.

Example
He put his arm around her when it started to _get_ dark.

a) I'm afraid I _____ no idea what you're talking about.

b) If you ever _____ an affair with someone, I will never speak to you again.

c) Let's not _____ a row about this; let's discuss it calmly.

d) More and more couples in Europe do not want to _____ children.

e) On their first evening together, they decided to _____ married.

f) One day, I'm going to _____ tired of all your questions.

g) They couldn't _____ divorced because of their religious beliefs.

4 Complete the phrasal verbs with *out* or *up*.

Example
This is the fourth time they have split _up_ , but they always get together again later.

a) Find _____ how much money he has before you say 'yes'!

b) I hate it when boys try to chat me _____ .

c) I'm much too shy to ask him _____ .

d) My boss is taking me _____ to an expensive restaurant.

e) Perhaps I'll ring him _____ and tell him it's over.

f) They stayed _____ all night watching romantic movies on the TV.

g) They went _____ together for twelve years before getting engaged.

Pronunciation

1 🔊 Listen to the recording and circle the word that you hear.

a) began / begun
b) drank / drunk
c) ran / run
d) rang / rung
e) sang / sung
f) sank / sunk
g) swam / swum

2 Look at the word *read* in the following sentences. How is it pronounced in each sentence?

a) I read the newspaper every morning before I go to work.

b) I read *War and Peace* last year.

c) Have you read the newspaper today?

🔊 Listen to the recording to check your answers.

Writing

Look at the pictures and write the story of Bonnie and Clyde. Use the questions to help you.

Begin the story like this:
Bonnie Parker was a waitress at Marco's Café in Rowena, Texas. One day she ...

Picture 1
Who did she meet?
What was he like?
Did Bonnie and Clyde fall in love at first sight?

Picture 2
Did Bonnie wear her best clothes the next day?
Where were Bonnie and Clyde walking?
What did Clyde see?

Picture 3
Did Bonnie and Clyde steal the car?
Where did they drive after this?

Picture 4
Who did Clyde point his gun at?
What was Bonnie doing while Clyde was taking the money?

Picture 5
Where did Bonnie and Clyde go one week later?
What did they do there?

Picture 6
Where did Bonnie and Clyde go three weeks later?
Why?
What happened when a policeman tried to arrest them?

Picture 7
What were Bonnie and Clyde doing six months later?
Where were the policemen?
Who were they waiting for?

Picture 8
Who fired their guns?
Who died?

BONNIE AND CLYDE

THEY WERE YOUNG ... THEY WERE IN LOVE ... AND THEY KILLED PEOPLE.

4 Fit

Grammar

1 Complete each sentence with the comparative form of the adjective in brackets.

Example
A salad is <u>healthier</u> (healthy) for you than a cheeseburger.

a) Healthy people are often _____ (happy) than people who are not fit.

b) It's _____ (hot) than yesterday, isn't it?

c) Michael Schumacher is a _____ (successful) racing driver than his brother.

d) Swimming is _____ (good) for your health than golf.

e) The nightlife in London is _____ (interesting) than in Oxford.

f) The pitch was _____ (big) than usual and the players were tired.

g) Your spelling is _____ (bad) than mine!

2 Solve the puzzle.

Daniel is fitter than David, but less fit than Jake. Lizzie is fitter than Daniel, but less fit than Jake. Rosa is fitter than all of them.

Put these five people in order of fitness.

the fittest _____

_____

_____

_____

the least fit _____

3 Complete each sentence with the superlative form of an adjective from the box.

| big | expensive | ~~heavy~~ | high | lucky |
| popular | rich | wet | | |

Example
<u>The heaviest</u> animal is the blue whale, which weighs about twenty-six tonnes.

a) _____ island in the world is Greenland (2 million km²).

b) _____ woman in the world won nearly $200 million in the Massachusetts Lottery.

c) 36–0 is _____ score in a professional football match.

d) At $466 million, the Stade de France was _____ stadium in the world when it was built.

e) Singapore is _____ place in the world with more than 200 centimetres of rain every year.

f) The Sumitomo Bank is _____ in the world.

g) With over 100,000 members of the fan club, Manchester United is _____ football team in England.

4 There is one word missing from each line in the text below. Insert the missing words. Choose from the words in the box. You can use them more than once.

| as | more | most | not | than | the |

Probably the ⁁most common health problem for men

is heart disease. Exercise is important, but not

important as a healthy diet. A bad diet is biggest

cause of this disease. Vegetables are better for you

fatty foods, but some vegetables are useful than

others. Supermarket products are as healthy as

organic produce. People with most stressful jobs

have shorter lives people who are stress-free. So

look for ways to relax. You should exercise more

once a week. A hard, sweaty sport is not good

for you regular, gentle exercise.

Listening and reading

1 📼 Cover the tapescript opposite and listen to part of a TV programme about sport. Match the sports in the pictures to the three stories.

2 📼 Listen to the programme again. Which sports personality are the following sentences talking about? Write your answers in the boxes:
SK – Shinzo Kanaguri; EM – Eric Moussambani;
EE – Eddie Edwards.

a) He came from Britain. ☐

b) He didn't enjoy taking part in his race. ☐

c) He needed to wear glasses. ☐

d) He took part in the Sydney Olympics. ☐

e) He stopped in the middle of the race. ☐

f) He only started the sport that year. ☐

g) He took part in the Stockholm Olympics.
☐

h) He broke some bones. ☐

i) He broke an Olympic record. ☐

j) They had a problem with the weather. ☐
☐

3 Look at the tapescript and choose the best definition of the words below, a) or b).

1 competitors (*line 7*)
   a) people taking part in a race
   b) people watching a race

2 blazing (*line 9*)
   a) very hot   b) very cold

3 disqualified (*line 22*)
   a) allowed to continue
   b) not allowed to continue

4 jaw (*line 43*)
   a) a bone of the face   b) a record

5 drops (*line 49*)
   a) jumps   b) falls

6 short-sighted (*line 54*)
   a) can see well   b) can't see well

Today we take a look at three of the greatest losers in the history of the Olympic Games. The first one was a certain Shinzo Kanaguri from Japan. He
5 ran in the 1912 Olympics in Stockholm. The marathon. It was an extremely hot day and, like all the other competitors, Shinzo was finding it extremely hard. As he was running along under the blazing
10 sun, he saw a family sitting at the side of the road having a picnic. They invited him to join them for their meal. After eating, he realised that there was little point in continuing with the race.

15 Number two is Eric Moussambani, also known as Eric the Eel. At the Sydney Olympics, Eric set a new Olympic record in the 100 metres freestyle. He won his race in the record slow time of 1 minute
20 52.72 seconds. There were two other swimmers in the race, but both of them were disqualified for false starts. Although he won the race, Eric's time was too slow to qualify for the final. His
25 time was just a little slower than the Olympic champion, Pieter van den Hoogenband, but van den Hoogenband swam 200 metres, compared to Eric's 100. Eric was just happy to finish his race
30 – it was his first time in a 50-metre pool and he had only taken up swimming a few months before.

My number three is Britain's very own sporting superstar, Eddie Edwards –
35 Eddie the Eagle. Eddie's chosen sport was a strange choice for a man who lives hundreds of miles from the nearest mountain. But at the Winter Olympics in Calgary, Eddie was the only member of
40 the British ski-jumping team, and he was entered for both the 70 and the 90 metre jumps. While he was preparing for the Olympics, he broke his jaw, his collarbone and a number of teeth. But
45 at Calgary, Eddie was ready – and came last in the 70 metre event. The Olympic officials did not want him to take part in the longer jump. 'The Eagle doesn't jump – he drops like a stone,' said one
50 Olympic official. But Eddie insisted and, once more, took last place – forty-seven metres behind the winner. At least he had a good excuse. Eddie the Eagle was very short-sighted and wore thick
55 glasses. In the cold mountain air, Eddie's glasses misted up and he couldn't see a thing.

Vocabulary

1 Complete the table. Use a dictionary if necessary.

sport	person	place
a) _____	boxer	ring
cycling	b) _____	velodrome/road
gymnastics	c) _____	gym
ice hockey	d) _____	rink
rowing	e) _____	river/lake
f) _____	skier	slope/piste
g) _____	squash player	court

2 Fill the gaps with *does*, *plays* or *goes*.

Trevor is a fitness freak. First thing in the morning, he either __goes__ for a run or (a) _____ swimming at the local pool. When he gets back, he (b) _____ the housework and then sets off for his job at the gym. It's the perfect job, because he (c) _____ weights and other exercises during his breaks. Three evenings a week, he (d) _____ squash with his best friend, and twice a week he (e) _____ karate. On Fridays he (f) _____ dancing with his friends from the gym. On Saturdays, he (g) _____ shopping in the morning, but in the afternoon he (h) _____ for a five-a-side football team. During the holidays, he usually (i) _____ windsurfing. It is, he says, the only way to stay beautiful.

3 Replace the underlined words with a word from the box.

attractive	average	calm	famous	fit
fortunate	fun	~~unhappy~~		

Example
Are you <u>sad</u> when your country loses a football match? *unhappy*

a) Are some gold medal winners at the Olympics very <u>lucky</u>?
b) Are the best tennis players always <u>cool</u> before a match?
c) Do you know any <u>good-looking</u> boxers?
d) Do you need to be <u>healthy</u> to play golf?
e) How much does the <u>typical</u> football player earn?
f) Which do you think are more <u>enjoyable</u>: team sports or individual sports?
g) Who is the most <u>well-known</u> sports personality in your country?

4 Make adjectives from the nouns in the box. Use the adjectives to complete the sentences.

aerobics	danger	~~interest~~	profession
success	sweat	talent	value

Example
Cricket is the least <u>interesting</u> sport in the world: nothing ever happens!

a) _____ basketball players can earn millions of dollars.
b) He's always very _____ after the match, so he has a shower.
c) It's important to do _____ exercise to keep fit.
d) Motor racing is a lot more _____ than golf.
e) Only the most _____ athletes win medals at the Olympics.
f) Real Madrid is probably the most _____ football club of all time.
g) Some football players' feet are extremely _____: they are insured for millions.

5 Match the phrases in box A with the words in box B to complete the expressions.

A

a)	He was as cold as
b)	His face was as white as
c)	It was as black as
d)	My face went as red as
e)	She's as slow as
f)	The children were as good as
g)	She was as quiet as

B

1	a beetroot
2	a mouse
3	a sheet
4	a tortoise
5	gold
6	ice
7	night

Writing

1 Rewrite the story below, using correct punctuation. You will need ten capital letters and ten full stops.

a man was feeling unwell and he went to see the doctor he went with his wife because he was a little worried afterwards the doctor spoke to the man's wife he said, 'I'm afraid I have some bad news unless you follow my instructions very carefully, your husband will die every morning you must give him a good breakfast and you must cook him a healthy meal at night what is more, you must not ask him to do any housework and you must keep the house very clean it is a lot of work for you, but it really is the only way to keep him alive'

on the way home, the husband asked his wife what the doctor had said to her 'he said you're going to die,' she replied

2 Correct the spelling mistakes in the story below.

One day a buss driver was in his buss when the bigest man he had ever seen got on. The giant looked at the driver, said, 'Big John doesn't pay,' and took his seet on the buss. The buss driver was only a litle man and he did not want to argue.

The next day, the same thing hapened. The man mountain got on the buss, looked at the driver and said, 'Big John doesn't pay.' Then, he went to a seet.

This hapened for sevral days. After a weak, the driver was begining to get a litle angry. Evrybody else payed, so why not the big man? So the driver went to a gym and began a course of body-bilding. He did not want to be frihgtened of Big John any more.

Two weaks later, the driver had strong mussles and was feelling very fit. At the usual stopp, Big John got on. 'Big John doesn't pay,' he said. But this time the driver was preppared for him. He got up and said, 'Oh, yeah? And why dosn't Big John pay?'

The man reached into his poket. For a momment, the driver was extremely scared. Perrhaps he had a gun? Then the man replyed, 'Becase Big John has got a buss pass.'

Pronunciation

1 How do you say the following numbers?

1 $63 million
   a) sixty-three million dollars
   b) sixty-three millions dollars
   c) dollars sixty-three million

2 47.75 km
   a) forty-seven point seventy-five kilometres
   b) forty-seven point seven five kilometres
   c) forty-seven comma seventy-five kilometres

3 6.6%
   a) six comma six per cent
   b) six point six per cent
   c) six comma six per cents

4 180 km/h
   a) a hundred eighty kilometres hour
   b) a hundred and eighty kilometres hour
   c) a hundred and eighty kilometres an hour

5 5–0 (football)
   a) five 'O' b) five nil c) five zero

6 2 ¾
   a) two and three fourths
   b) two and three quarter
   c) two and three quarters

7 0.675
   a) nought point six seven five
   b) nought point six hundred and seventy five
   c) nought point sixty-seven five

Listen to the recording to check your answers.

2 The words below all have three syllables. Do they have the stress on the first or the second syllable? Put them into the correct column.

advertise   attractive   certainly
cheeseburger   marathon   opinion
percentage   photograph   statistics
surprising   tournament   wonderful

Ooo	oOo
advertise	attractive

Listen to the recording to check your answers.

5 *Review 1*

Grammar

1 Put the words in the box into one of the three categories (*verbs*, *nouns* or *adjectives*) in column A. Then complete column B.

> ~~bad~~ ~~beach~~ ~~become~~ catch child
> choose church clever draw fall
> fancy foot lucky meet mouse
> pay sad send shy thin tooth
> ugly university wet win

A

verbs

become _____

catch _____

_____

_____

_____

_____

_____

_____

_____

nouns

beach _____

_____

_____

_____

_____

_____

adjectives

bad _____

_____

_____

_____

_____

_____

B

past tense

became _____

ca _____

_____

_____

_____

_____

_____

_____

_____

plural

beaches _____

_____

_____

_____

_____

_____

comparative

worse _____

_____

_____

_____

_____

_____

2 Rearrange the words to make questions.

Example
any children got Have you ?
Have you got any children?

a) best did friend meet When you your ?

_____

b) class in is person tallest the Who your ?

_____

c) country in is like the weather What your ?

_____

d) day do emails every get How many you ?

_____

e) does teacher like look What your ?

_____

f) wearing were What yesterday you ?

_____

3 Each of the sentences below has *one* word missing. Insert the missing words.

Example   do
What names/you like for a boy?

a) He drinks far much beer.

b) How your parents choose your name?

c) It raining when I arrived at work.

d) There were lot of people at the disco.

e) Tiger Woods is greatest golfer of all time.

f) Venus Williams isn't as tall Shaquille O'Neal.

g) What the shops like in your home town?

4 Circle the best alternative.

'Wake up, darling, it's a beautiful morning,' said Mrs Everest.

'Ughh,' replied her husband. 'Why *did you wake* / *woke you* me? I (a) *slept* / *was sleeping*.'

'It's (b) *more* / *the most* beautiful day of the year. Why (c) *don't we go* / *we not go* to the country and get some fresh (d) *air* / *airs*? If we leave now, there won't be (e) *much* / *many* traffic.'

A (f) *few* / *little* hours later, Mr Everest was finally ready. They (g) *got* / *were getting* into the car and set off. At twelve o'clock, they (h) *drove* / *were driving* along a country road when Mr Everest (i) *saw* / *was seeing* a country pub. 'That (j) *looks* / *looks like* nice. Why (k) *don't we* / *we don't* stop there for lunch?'

After a long lunch, they (l) *got* / *were getting* back into the car and (m) *continued* / *were continuing* their journey. After another hour, Mrs Everest (n) *turned* / *was turning* to her husband and (o) *said* / *was saying* nervously, 'Darling, I think I (p) *left* / *was leaving* my handbag in the pub.' Her husband (q) *looked* / *looked like* really angry. 'Typical, typical…' he said under his breath.

When (r) *did they get* / *they got* back to the pub, he was still angry. 'It's already four o'clock,' he said. 'We haven't got (s) *enough time* / *time enough* to go to the country now. What a waste of time!'

Mrs Everest got out of the car and was walking towards the pub when her husband (t) *stopped* / *was stopping* her.

'I almost forgot. (u) *Can you ask* / *Do you can ask* them if they have got my hat?'

5 Rewrite the sentences beginning with the words given.

Example
Have you got any children?
Do you *have any children?*

a) What's your weight?
How much _____

b) There were only a few people at the party.
There were not _____

c) I didn't get much sleep last night.
I didn't get a _____

d) She has known him for two years.
She met _____

e) What clothes did you have on yesterday?
What were _____

f) Michael isn't as attractive as Raúl.
Raúl is _____

g) Inge is older than Cathy.
Cathy isn't _____

h) There isn't a golfer in the world who is better than Tiger Woods.
Tiger Woods is the _____

6 Find a response in box B to the sentences in box A.

A

a) Are you interested in football?
b) How long does it take you to do your homework?
c) How often do you go to the gym?
d) Is there anything you don't like about your job?
e) What do you have in common with your sister?
f) What's up? Are you all right?
g) What's your favourite song by Celine Dion?
h) What's your new teacher like?

B

1 Not really. I split up with my boyfriend last night.
2 Everything! She even looks like me.
3 It depends. Sometimes a quarter of an hour, sometimes longer.
4 No, not at all. I think it's perfect.
5 Not really. I've never been to a match in my life.
6 Oh, once or twice a week usually.
7 She's lovely and her lessons are fantastic.
8 Who? Never heard of her!

Vocabulary

1 Look at the picture and say if the sentences are true (T) or false (F).

Example

A couple are sightseeing and taking

photographs. ☐ T

a) The couple are middle-aged. ☐

b) They are having a row. ☐

c) The woman is standing in front of a statue. ☐

d) She has blond hair and a big smile. ☐

e) There is a café on the other side of the canal. ☐

f) The café does not have a good view of the canal because of the traffic. ☐

g) A nurse in uniform is sitting at the café. ☐

h) There is an old bridge over the canal. ☐

i) A man in a boat is using his mobile phone. ☐

j) He does not look very fit. ☐

k) There is a castle next to the café. ☐

l) Most of the architecture of the town is very modern. ☐

2 Complete the sentences with *down*, *out* or *up*.

Example

We need to find <u>out</u> what time the train leaves.

a) He's completely stressed _____ about his new job.

b) I met this horrible guy yesterday who tried to chat me _____ .

c) I think I'll stay _____ and watch the late night movie on TV.

d) I thought you were never going to ask me _____ .

e) Listen carefully and write _____ the words you hear.

f) She was born and grew _____ in the south of Egypt.

g) They split _____ when he met someone else.

h) Why don't you ring me _____ this evening and we'll talk about it?

3 Put the missing words in the grid below to find the hidden words in the grey boxes.

Example

He was so ...... ! I've never seen anyone so unattractive!

a) The children were really ...... – we couldn't hear ourselves speak.

b) I need to ...... my English – it's not good enough.

c) The athletes were on the ...... waiting for the race to begin.

d) The Prime Minister died yesterday and his ...... will be next week.

e) When did Alexander Bell ...... the telephone?

f) They live in a small ...... with a population of about a hundred people.

g) In her new job, she will ...... about sixty thousand dollars a year.

	U	G	L	Y		
a)		O			Y	
b)		M				E
c)		R		K		
d)		U				L
e)		N			T	
f)		I				E
g)		A		N		

4 Circle the best alternative.

Example

Does he never (get) / have / make tired of talking?

a) Do you get / have / make a lot in common with your sister?

b) I get / have / make no idea what you are talking about.

c) I think he's getting / having / making an affair with his secretary.

d) I'm tired – let's get / have / make a taxi.

e) It's time to get / have / make a decision – what do you think?

f) They got / had / made married just after they left school.

g) What time does it get / have / make dark in August?

h) You can improve your memory if you learn to get / have / make different associations.

i) You have to get / have / make a choice – it's your work or me!

5 Make nouns from the following words.

Example

choose _____choice_____

a) dangerous _____

b) decide _____

c) describe _____

d) fashionable _____

e) introduce _____

f) lucky _____

g) marry _____

h) noisy _____

i) operate _____

j) religious _____

k) romantic _____

l) succeed _____

6 Complete each sentence with a noun from exercise 5.

Example

Good <u>luck</u> with your exam tomorrow.

a) Can you give us a _____ of the person who stole your money?

b) For the first course, you have a _____ between soup or salad.

c) He had to go into hospital for an _____ on his back.

d) His first film was a great _____ and won four Oscars.

e) People who drink and drive are a _____ on the roads.

f) They had an unhappy _____ and separated after a few years.

g) What colour is in _____ this summer?

h) Your written homework needs an _____ , a middle and a conclusion.

7 Replace the words in *italics* with their opposites from the box and rewrite the story. You may need to change *a* to *an*.

boring	cheap	difficult	least	poor
terrible	unattractive	~~unusual~~	worst	

I went out on a *typical* date with my boyfriend yesterday. He took me to a very *expensive* restaurant and I had the *best* meal of my life. The food was *fantastic* and the wine was the *most* expensive on the menu. John is an *easy* man to be with: he's *rich*, *good-looking* and he can be very *amusing*. When he asked me to marry him, I said ...

I went out on an unusual date with .... .

_____

_____

_____

_____

_____

_____

_____

_____

_____

_____

8 Find and correct twelve spelling mistakes in the story below.

One day, a man didn't come home from work. The next morning he still wasn't there so his wife went to the police. They asked her to describe her husbend's apearance. 'He's 38, avrage hieght, he's extreemly good-looking, with a moustashe, dark hair, athletic build, and he looks very inteligent.'

Later in the day, her freind said, 'Why did you say that? He's the compleat oposite. He's very short, overwieght, and has a face like a cheesburger!'

'I know,' said the wife, 'but I don't want the police to bring *him* back.'

husband's

_____ _____ _____

_____ _____ _____

_____ _____ _____

_____ _____ _____

6 Shop

Grammar

1 Complete the sentences with *for* or *to*.

Example
I think I'll buy some perfume _for_ my grandmother.

a) I told your secret _____ my husband – I hope that's okay.

b) I've lent my car _____ my sister.

c) Philip made a delicious meal _____ his girlfriend.

d) Why don't you get some chocolates _____ your mother?

e) You need to show your bus pass _____ the driver.

f) Give the ticket _____ the receptionist.

g) I sent a letter _____ the bank manager last week.

2 Rewrite the sentences in exercise 1. Replace the words in *italics* with a pronoun (*him* or *her*) and do not use *for* or *to*.

Example
I think I'll buy her some perfume.

a) _____
b) _____
c) _____
d) _____
e) _____
f) _____
g) _____

3 Some of the sentences below contain a word that should not be there. Cross out the unnecessary words. Four sentences are correct.

Example
She told ~~to~~ me all about her new job.

a) I'm going to write a letter to you very soon.

b) She sent the tickets to the wrong address.

c) I gave for my nephew a gold pen on his birthday.

d) We've brought to you some really good news.

e) He is teaching history to first-year students this year.

f) Can I show my photos to you one day?

g) The shop assistant explained me the advantages of speed dialling.

h) She described us the new leopard-skin mini-skirt she had bought.

4 Rearrange the words to make sentences.

Example
a always diet is on She
She is always on a diet.

a) drives He mad me often

_____

b) ever hardly I perfume wear

_____

c) arrive doesn't She on time usually

_____

d) a been centre garden have I never to

_____

e) about her husband is positive rarely She

_____

f) celebrate Day don't We often Valentine's

_____

g) am at presents good I normally not choosing very

_____

5 Complete each sentence with an appropriate form of the verb in brackets.

Example
He really hates _getting up_ (get up) in the morning.

a) He often decides _____ (stay) in bed all day.

b) He enjoys _____ (spend) the evening in front of the TV.

c) He wastes hours _____ (surf) the net.

d) He doesn't mind _____ (eat) take-aways every day.

e) He doesn't need _____ (look) for a job.

f) He wants _____ (have) a life of leisure.

g) He spends his summers _____ (go) to free festivals.

Reading

1 Look at the newspaper article opposite. The article contains a mistake. One sentence does not belong. Find the sentence and cross it out.

2 Choose the best answer.

1 What is special about the shop *Out of the Closet*?
   a) It is in London's fashionable Bond Street.
   b) All of the clothes are of very high quality.
   c) The clothes are all old.
   d) The clothes in it all belonged to Elton John.

2 Why is Elton John selling his old clothes?
   a) Because he doesn't like them any more.
   b) Because he wants to make money for a charity.
   c) Because his wardrobe is too small.
   d) Because his wardrobe is empty.

3 Why did Elton John spend so much money?
   a) Because he was growing up.
   b) Because he was living in Britain.
   c) Because he was a shopaholic.
   d) Because he bought a lot of flowers.

4 What kind of people suffer most from oniomania?
   a) Americans.
   b) Pop stars.
   c) Women.
   d) Psychologists.

5 Why is oniomania more of a problem now than in the past?
   a) Because Elton John is very popular.
   b) Because psychologists have known about the problem for a long time.
   c) Because there are more shops and it is easy to get credit.
   d) Because there are more and more drink and drug addicts.

6 Why do some scientists think that people are shopaholics?
   a) Because they get expensive presents instead of love when they are young.
   b) Because they spend too much time with their parents.
   c) Because they have taken an anti-depressant drug.
   d) Because they haven't got any scissors.

Shop till you drop

On Wednesday of next week, shoppers in London's fashionable Bond Street will be able to buy something special. Wednesday sees the opening of *Out of the Closet*, a clothes shop with a difference. All of the items on sale are of the highest quality: beautiful silk shirts, Versace sweaters, crocodile skin shoes... But what makes these clothes so special is that they belonged to Elton John. He is selling his old clothes to make money for a charity that helps AIDS victims. But even when everything has been sold, his wardrobe will not be empty. Elton John is one of the growing number of 'shopaholics' in Britain. One year he spent £25 million, including £300,000 on flowers and £9 million on property.

It is estimated that 15 million people in the US suffer from the same problem as Elton John. The technical name for this disorder is 'oniomania' and nine out of ten sufferers are women.

Psychologists have known about the problem for a long time. But the opening of more and more shopping centres and the easy availability of credit cards has changed everything. It's often a good idea to try on one or two pairs. There are now more shopaholics than drink or drug addicts in the UK. Many have serious financial problems, but the condition also results in family break-ups, homelessness and suicide.

Scientists are trying to find out why some people enjoy shopping so much. One idea is that it is connected to problems during childhood. Many parents do not have much time to spend with their children. Instead of love and affection, they buy their children expensive presents, and the child associates shopping with security and pleasure.

Fortunately, there are cures for the condition. Many people feel better when they spend money, but psychotherapy can help shopaholics discover why they are unhappy in the first place. For others, anti-depressant drugs may help. But the best cure is probably to take your credit cards out of your wallet and cut them up. Remember: one pair of scissors is enough.

Vocabulary

1 Combine a word from box A with a word from box B to make compound nouns. Then use them to complete the sentences below.

A	B
~~birthday~~	assistant
mobile	bag
electronic	dress
engagement	gadget
shopping	~~present~~
price	ring
shop	phone
evening	tag

Example
For my <u>birthday present</u> last year, Aunt Susan gave me a pair of socks.

a) I'm going to a formal dinner next week and I need to buy a new _____ .

b) It was a diamond _____ and she couldn't understand where he had found the money to buy it.

c) The _____ broke, the bottle fell out and smashed on the floor.

d) The _____ was young and inexperienced and couldn't help me at all.

e) Nokia is one of the best-known makes of _____ .

f) These trousers normally cost £40 but the _____ was wrong and I only had to pay £25.

g) My father always wants to buy the latest _____ .

2 Put the following words under the correct heading.

~~check~~   ~~cotton~~   denim   leather
patterned   plain   silk   striped
synthetic   woollen

material	*pattern*
cotton	check
_____	_____
_____	_____
_____	_____
_____	_____

3 Label the pictures. The first letter of each word has been given to you.

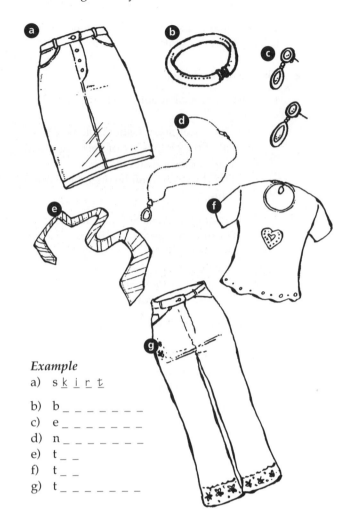

Example
a) s <u>k</u> <u>i</u> <u>r</u> <u>t</u>

b) b _ _ _ _ _ _ _
c) e _ _ _ _ _ _ _
d) n _ _ _ _ _ _ _
e) t _ _
f) t _ _
g) t _ _ _ _ _ _ _

4 Match the questions in box A with their answers in box B.

A

a) Can I have a refund if my wife doesn't like it?
b) Can I help you, madam?
c) Did you give me the receipt?
d) Do you take credit cards?
e) Do you think this dress suits me?
f) Have you got anything more brightly coloured?
g) Is it the right size, madam?
h) Would you like to try on something else?

B

1 No, but we have this nice blue one.
2 No, but you can always exchange it.
3 No, I'm sorry, here you are.
4 No, I'm sorry, just cash or cheques.
5 No, it doesn't fit at all!
6 No, thanks, I'll take this one.
7 No, thanks, I'm just looking.
8 No, you look like a sack of potatoes.

Writing

Fill in the online registration form for an online shopping service.

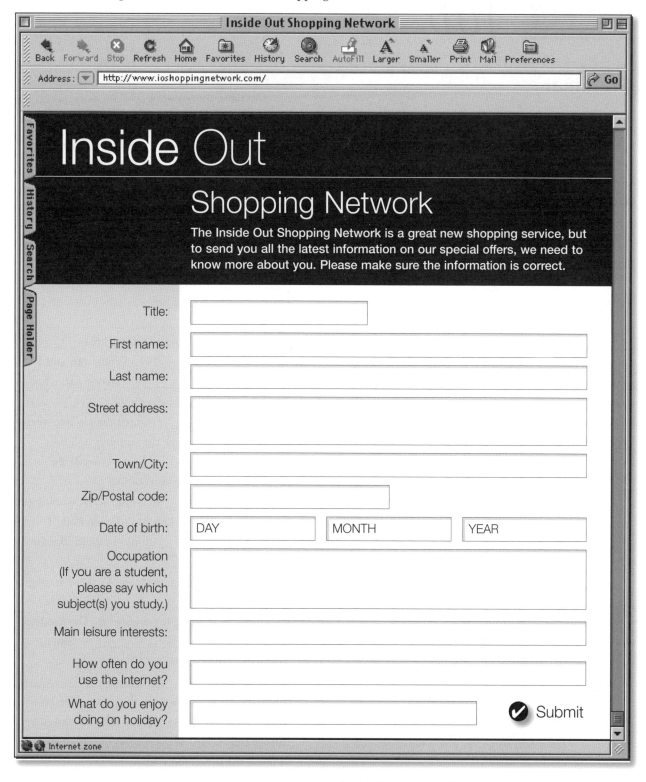

Pronunciation

Insert *and* into the numbers opposite, where you need to say 'and'. An example has been done for you.

Example

and   and

2̷8 5, 7̷5 0

a) 9 2 5

b) 2,9 4 0

c) 1 3,8 2 2

d) 1 1 8,7 5 0

e) 2,7 5 0,6 0 5

f) 5 0,0 0 0,4 2 9

g) 9 9 9,9 9 9,9 9 9

Listen to the recording to check your answers.

7 Job

Grammar

1 Complete the table. Use your dictionary if you need help.

infinitive	past simple	past participle
break	_____	_____
cut	_____	_____
drop	_____	_____
hold	_____	_____
know	_____	_____
leave	_____	_____
pay	_____	_____
run	_____	_____
see	_____	_____
stand	_____	_____
tell	_____	_____
travel	_____	_____
try	_____	_____

2 Put the verbs into the present perfect tense.

Example
How many different jobs _has she done_ (she do)?

a) She _____ (have) dozens of jobs in her life.

b) _____ (you ever work) in a factory?

c) No, I _____ (never be) in a factory.

d) What's the worst thing that _____ (ever happen) to you in a job?

e) I _____ (hate) most of my jobs and I hate this one too.

f) _____ (you ever think) of running your own business?

g) Yes, I _____ (always want) to be my own boss.

3 Circle the best time expression.

Example
Did you learn to drive (when you were 18) / ever / in your life ?

a) Have you been to the cinema *a few weeks ago / last week / this week* ?

b) I bought a great CD *in my life / over the years / yesterday.*

c) I didn't go to the beach at all *last summer / over the years / recently.*

d) So far, I've been to a restaurant twice *last Friday / never / this week.*

e) I've done a lot of silly things *a few years ago / last year / over the years.*

f) I've met a lot of interesting people *last year / recently / when I was a student.*

g) I've spent far too much money *last night / today / yesterday.*

4 Put the verbs in brackets into either the past simple or the present perfect.

I _have done_ (do) lots of horrible jobs in my life, but the worst job I (a) _____ (ever have) was selling hot dogs. I (b) _____ (always be) a vegetarian and I (c) _____ (never eat) a hot dog in my life. And I never will!
I (d) _____ (start) the job two years ago at the beginning of the summer holidays because I (e) _____ (need) the money to pay for my studies. We (f) _____ (have) to sell the hotdogs from little trolleys in London's Green Park. I (g) _____ (think) I would like the job, because I (h)_____ (always like) working outdoors. I was so wrong! I (i) _____ (never make) such a big mistake in my whole life. The hotdogs and the onions (j) _____ (smell) disgusting, the customers (k) _____ (be) rude and we (l) _____ (often have) problems with the police. The boss (m) _____ (be) a big, fat man in a leather jacket. He (n) _____ (shout) at us all the time. 'How many (o) _____ (you sell) today? You (p) _____ (not sell) enough!' One day, the police (q) _____ (arrest) him and that (r) _____ (be) the end of the job. I (s) _____ (never be) so happy in my whole life!

Listening

1  Cover the tapescripts opposite and listen to two people playing a game. One person thinks of a job and the other person has to guess what it is. Tick (✓) the two jobs that are described.

a) a dishwasher

b) a waiter

c) a chef

d) a lifeguard

e) a conductor

f) a pilot

2 Listen to the people playing the game a third time. They ask the same questions as in the first game, but the answers are different. Write down the answers (*Yes* or *No*) as you listen.

a) Do you work indoors?
b) Do you use your hands in this job?
c) Is it a well-paid job?
d) Do you need any qualifications for this job?
e) What hours do you work? No, hang on, do you work normal office hours?
f) Do you have to work in the evenings?
g) Do you have to wear a uniform?
h) Is it a hot and smelly job?
i) I think I've got it. Do you work in a restaurant?
j) I know. You're a waiter!
k) Okay, so you're a chef?

3 Look at the pictures again. Can you guess which job is being described?

A: So, do you work indoors or outdoors?
B: I can only say 'yes' or 'no'.
A: Okay, do you work indoors?
B: Yes.
A: Do you use your hands in this job?
B: Yes.
A: Is it a well-paid job?
B: Erm, no, not usually.
A: Do you need any qualifications for this job?
B: Yes. Usually.
A: What hours do you work? No, hang on, do you work normal office hours?
B: No.
A: Do you have to work in the evenings?
B: Yes.
A: Do you have to wear a uniform?
B: Yes.
A: Is it a hot and smelly job?
B: Er, yes, I suppose so.
A: I think I've got it. Do you work in a restaurant?
B: Yes.
A: I know. You're a waiter!
B: No!
A: Okay, so you're a chef?
B: Yes, you've got it.

B: Okay, my turn. Is it a job for men or women? I mean, do men usually do this job?
A: Yes, men, usually.
B: Do you have to be strong?
A: No! Not at all.
B: Do you need any special tools?
A: Yes, one. One special tool. A sort of tool, I suppose.
B: Do you work in an office?
A: No.
B: Is it an artistic job?
A: Yes.
B: Do you work in a studio?
A: Yes, sometimes.
B: Painter!
A: No.
B: Oh. Er, I don't know. Do you travel a lot in this job?
A: Quite a lot.
B: A pilot? No, no, that's not artistic. Do you wear a uniform?
A: Yes, sort of. Special clothes.
B: Oh, I don't know. Is it something to do with music?
A: Yes!
B: Do you play an instrument?
A: No.
B: Are you a – you know – a conductor?
A: Yes. At last!

Vocabulary

1 Search the word square (↑ ↓ → ←) for seventeen jobs.

P	H	O	T	O	G	R	A	P	H	E	R
T	A	Y	R	A	T	E	R	C	E	S	W
N	I	T	E	V	R	R	I	A	P	U	A
A	R	A	C	T	O	R	C	H	E	F	I
T	D	R	C	B	T	A	R	T	I	S	T
N	R	E	M	A	C	R	A	R	Y	E	R
U	E	H	E	N	O	N	U	R	S	E	E
O	S	C	E	K	D	P	I	L	O	T	S
C	S	A	N	E	F	I	W	D	I	M	S
C	E	E	E	R	A	N	T	R	E	L	S
A	R	T	R	E	M	R	A	F	L	A	S

accountant _____ _____

au pair _____ _____

artist _____ _____

_____ _____

_____ _____

_____ _____

_____ _____

_____

2 Complete each sentence with a word from the box.

> application   career   company
> employee   living   notice   salary   staff

a) He wanted to have a _____ in the police force, but he failed the entrance exam.

b) I don't want to be an _____ any more. I want to work for myself.

c) Most of the _____ in the restaurant are unhappy with their pay.

d) She's handed in her _____ and she's leaving in four weeks.

e) The job is really interesting but the _____ is terrible.

f) What does he do for a _____ ? He's a secret agent!

g) What sort of _____ do you work for?

h) When we receive your _____ , we will contact you for an interview.

3 Find a response in box B to the sentences in box A.

A

> a) I've just bought a new car.
> b) OK, so, exercises 1, 2, 3, 5, 7, 8 and 9 for homework.
> c) The children are going to stay with their grandparents next week.
> d) How do you change a nappy? I've never done it before.
> e) I've got a problem with my computer.
> f) My job is really boring.

B

> 1 Yes, but on the other hand it's very well paid.
> 2 So, you'll have a lot of time on your hands?
> 3 Well, you'll have to get a pen and paper and do it by hand!
> 4 What – new or second-hand?
> 5 When shall we hand it in?
> 6 Would you like me to give you a hand?

4 Complete the questions with a past participle. Some letters have been given to you.

Example
Do you know anyone who has r u n their own business?

a) Have you ever b r _ _ _ _ the law?

b) Have you ever g i _ _ _ a speech at a wedding?

c) Have you ever w o _ _ _ _ nights?

d) How many days off have you h _ _ in the last six months?

e) How much money have you e a _ _ _ _ this year?

f) What's the worst job you've ever d _ _ _ ?

g) What's the worst thing that has ever h a _ _ _ _ _ _ to you?

Pronunciation

🔊 Look at the text below. Practise reading it while you listen to the recording.

Hi. //
My name's Frank, //
and I come from / Bern / in Switzerland. //
I work‿as‿an artist for‿an on-line language school,
//but I also teach German and English. //
I've been with the company for‿a couple‿of years //
and I enjoy my work. //

Writing

1 Look at the advertisement below and put the parts of the letter in the correct places.

London Job Placements

Work in London in your summer holidays

We are looking for hundreds of people for temporary jobs in London: restaurants, shops, offices, au pairs, summer camps, travel guides, building sites ...

Good rates of pay and help with accommodation provided.

Send us a short letter, telling us

a when you are available for work,

b what work experience you have, enclosing a full CV, and

c what kind of work you prefer.

Send to: Emily Evans, London Job Placements, P.O. Box 414B, London ES7 4QR

a) 6th July 2002

b) I am writing in reply to your advertisement in International Travel Monthly

c) I am a third-year engineering student at the University of Leioa, near Bilbao.

d) I am available for work this summer in the months of July and August.

e) Please see my CV for further details.

f) Yours sincerely,

g) I have experience of working in restaurants and offices. I have also worked with children.

h) *Iñaki Rosel*

i) Basagoiti, 79, 10⁰, 48990 Berango Spain

j) I look forward to hearing from you.

k) I would prefer a job where I could practise my English, but I would be happy to consider any offer.

l) Iñaki Rosel

m) Dear Ms Evans,

n) Emily Evans, London Job Placements, P.O. Box 414B, London ES7 4QR

	1 i
2	**3**
4	
5	
6, 7	
8, 9, 10	
11	
12	
13	
14	

2 Use the letter above as a model and write your own reply to the advertisement.

8 *Rich*

Grammar

1 Correct the grammatical mistake in each sentence.

Example

What ~~we are~~ *are we* going to do tonight, Veronica?

a) I'm tired. I going to have an early night.

b) What about tomorrow? Are you go to be free in the evening?

c) Yes, but I not am going to go out. I want to watch TV.

d) Are you going come with me to my parents on Saturday?

e) No, I'm going to seeing Tony and Carla at the weekend.

f) Veronica, when are we going get married?

g) I've already told you, Barry. We're never to going get married.

2 Look at the sentences below. Does the present continuous refer to the present (P) and or to the future (F)?

Example

Are you enjoying your English classes?   P

a) European finance ministers are meeting in Frankfurt on Friday.

b) He's doing three concerts in Germany and two in Italy.

c) I'm feeling really great, thank you.

d) She's getting a lot of attention because of her new album.

e) They're moving into their new house at the weekend.

f) This is John Simpson of BBC World and I'm speaking from the Uzbek capital of Tashkent.

g) We're having a party on Saturday. Would you like to come?

3 Look at Matt McKay's list of appointments for Tuesday and write sentences using the present continuous. Use the verbs in the box.

| attend | fly | give | have | ~~meet~~ |

TUESDAY

10.00 Bank manager

13.00 Lunch with Mum

15.00 Interview (MTV studios)

18.00 Heathrow – Dublin

20.00 Music Monthly Awards Ceremony

Example

He's meeting his bank manager at 10 o'clock.

a) _____

b) _____

c) _____

d) _____

4 Rearrange the words to make questions. Then answer the questions.

Example

are bed go going time to to tonight What you ?

What time are you going to go to bed tonight?
Answer: *I'm going to bed at midnight.*

a) are for going have lunch to tomorrow What you ?

_____

_____

Answer: _____

_____

b) after are do going lesson the to What you ?

_____

_____

Answer: _____

_____

c) are do going this to weekend What you ?

_____

_____

Answer: _____

_____

Reading

1 Choose the best headline for the newspaper article opposite.

- **Getty becomes British**
- **Getty helps troubled Conservative Party**
- **Getty's son kidnapped by Mafia**
- **National Gallery gets £50 million**

2 Read the article again and decide if the following sentences are true (T) or false (F).

a) Getty often donates money to political parties. ☐

b) Getty's father made his money from oil. ☐

c) The Conservative Party has recently changed its leader. ☐

d) Getty doesn't like the British way of life. ☐

e) Getty gave £50 million to the British Film Institute. ☐

f) Last year, he gave £1 million to a homeless drug addict. ☐

g) His last wife died of drugs. ☐

h) Getty cut his son's ear off. ☐

i) Getty became religious later in his life. ☐

j) The British government was Conservative when the article was written. ☐

3 Complete the sentences below with words from the article opposite. The first letter of each word has been given to you.

a) Which p_____ did you vote for in the last election? (*paragraph 1*)

b) Have you ever d_____ anything to charity? (*paragraph 1*)

c) I am very g_____ to my parents for helping me in so many ways. (*paragraph 1*)

d) It's a special hospital that looks after drug a_____ and alcoholics. (*paragraph 2*)

e) Terrorists have k_____ the son of the President and are asking for $10 million. (*paragraph 3*)

f) I hope you haven't changed your m_____ about helping me. (*paragraph 3*)

g) She inherited an absolute f_____ from her grandmother. (*paragraph 4*)

h) The teacher h_____ back the homework the next day. (*paragraph 5*)

The Conservative Party announced today that it had received £5 million from the millionaire, John Paul Getty II. This is the first time that Getty has donated money to a political party. Getty, who is the son of an American oil billionaire, described his love for 'the British way of life'. In a statement, he said, 'I hope that my donation will help to enable the new leader to deliver a Conservative victory at the next election.' The Conservatives, after a disastrous last election and long arguments about a new leader, will be grateful for all the help they can get.

Getty is famous for giving away enormous amounts of money. A number of years ago, he gave £50 million to the National Gallery and £20 million to the British Film Institute. In addition, each year, he gives away more than £1 million to drug addicts, the homeless and other people in need. 'As long as I have money, I will give it away,' he once said.

His private life has been full of drama. He has been married three times – his second wife died of drugs. His son was kidnapped by the Mafia, and the grandfather refused to pay. Getty Senior changed his mind when one of the boy's ears was cut off and sent to a news-paper.

After years of wild living, Getty discovered God and converted to Catholicism. At the same time, he learnt that a reorganisation of the family fortune had left him with £300 million. He created a charity to manage the distribution of his money.

In 1998 he handed back his American pass-port and became a British citizen. He admits that the Britain he loves (the Britain of cricket and warm beer) is not the Britain that exists today. Will the Conservative Party be able to return Britain to the romantic past? They will need to win an election first.

Vocabulary

1 Circle the best alternative.

Example
We don't take credit cards, we only take
money / (cash) / fortune.

a) He *inherited / interested / invested* some money
   from his grandmother and bought a new
   house with it.
b) I must remember to pay the electricity
   account / bill / tax this week!
c) The *pension / profit / rent* for an apartment in
   the city centre is extremely high.
d) They made a big *cash / profit / salary* from the
   sale of their house.
e) We want to buy a new car, so we try to
   inherit / lend / save some money every month.
f) What's the *currency / exchange rate / worth* for
   the dollar?
g) When she retired, her *pension / salary / value*
   wasn't enough to live on.
h) Why don't you *earn / grow / invest* some of
   your money instead of spending it all?
i) She doesn't *earn / win / manage* much, but she
   likes the job.

2 Complete the story with words from the box.

band	single	cancelled	charts
concert	fans	gigs	lead	album	tour

In 1976, the punk (a) _____ , the Sex
Pistols, recorded their first (b) _____ ,
Anarchy in the UK. Although they had a few
(c) _____ , the Sex Pistols were not
famous until they appeared on TV in December
of that year. The record company, EMI,
(d) _____ the group's contract because of
the disgusting things they said on the TV
programme. With a new record company, their
next record, *God Save the Queen*, went to the top
of the (e) _____ but it was banned by the
BBC because it criticised the Queen. On the day
of the Queen's silver anniversary, the group
organised a (f) _____ on a boat on the
River Thames, but they were arrested by the
police. After three more hits, they brought out all
their songs on an (g) _____ , which was
also very successful. There were more problems
with the police, and many towns banned
(h) _____ by the group. After a short
(i) _____ of the U.S., the (j) _____
singer, Johnny Rotten, decided to leave.

3 Match the sentence beginnings in box A with their endings in box B.

A

a) At the end of the concert, they gave
b) He wants to give
c) It's very difficult to come
d) She has always wanted to go
e) The concert was sold
f) The group decided to split
g) The group's new record is coming
h) They only had one hit, but they carried

B

1 out next week.
2 on making records for fifteen years.
3 away free T-shirts.
4 out two weeks ago.
5 out with a rock star.
6 up after two years together.
7 up his job in the bank and join a band.
8 up with an original idea for a pop video.

4 Complete each sentence by making a noun from the word in brackets.

Example
The thieves stole his *collection* (collect) of antique
furniture.

a) Matt announced his _____ (decide)
   to pursue a solo career.
b) Our last holiday was a complete
   _____ (disastrous).
c) Many mothers look for part-time
   _____ (employ) when their children
   are young.
d) Mandela finally won his _____ (free)
   after twenty-six years in prison.
e) The singer was given a bouquet of roses at
   the end of the _____ (perform).
f) It is hard to explain the _____
   (popular) of some pop bands.
g) They are going to buy a house by the sea for
   their _____ (retire).
h) The band bought a new van to transport all
   their _____ (equip).

Writing

1 Where do the phrases below belong in the letter? Write the number in the box.

a) Could you please tell me ☐

b) Finally, I would appreciate it if you could send me ☐

c) First of all, I would like to know a little more about ☐

d) For instance ☐

e) I am writing with reference to ☐ 1

f) I look forward to hearing from you soon. ☐

g) I would be grateful if you would send me ☐

h) In addition, I would appreciate more information about ☐

Dear Sir/Madam,

....(1).... your advertisement in the newspaper yesterday. I am interested in applying to the Trust and ....(2).... further information.

....(3).... the Trust. Your advertisement says that it is for young people. ....(4).... how old I must be to apply? I am going to be 18 next month. ....(5).... the kinds of projects that you support. ....(6).... , is it possible to receive a grant to help with my university studies?

....(7).... an application form.

....(8).... .

Yours faithfully,

Cosmo Brickett

Cosmo Brickett

---

2 Look at the advertisement and notes and write a letter asking for more information.

What kind of work?   Travel – who pays?

VOLUNTARY
Work Camps

Learn new skills and a new language at our international voluntary work camps

Our volunteer work program offers a huge range of possibilities to responsible young people who want to discover the world and make it a better place to live.

Your accommodation will be in our dormitories and all meals are provided.

Places available in our programmes starting July, September and January.

Don't delay – apply today!

Write to:

How long are the work camps?

Pronunciation

1 Read these song titles aloud, changing *going to* to *gonna*.

a) Who's going to stop the rain?   (Anastacia)
b) Your time is going to come   (Led Zeppelin)
c) I'm going to be alright   (Jennifer Lopez)
d) It's going to be me   (N'Sync)

▭▭ Repeat the song titles after the recording.

2 ▭▭ Now listen to these song titles. What is *wanna* short for?

I wanna be your man   (The Beatles)
Scream if you wanna go faster   (Geri Halliwell)
I wanna dance with somebody who loves me
 (Whitney Houston)
Wanna get paid   (LL Cool J)

9 *Rules*

Grammar

1 For each situation below, tick (✓) the correct consequence.

Example
Emma's English teacher was ill.
a) Emma didn't have to go to school that morning. ✓
b) Emma couldn't go to school that morning.

1 *The next day was a holiday.*
  a) She didn't have to go to work.
  b) She couldn't go to work.

2 *She wanted to go out, but her telephone wasn't working.*
  a) She didn't have to telephone anyone.
  b) She couldn't telephone anyone.

3 *Her best friend was in America on holiday.*
  a) She didn't have to go and see her.
  b) She couldn't go and see her.

4 *It was too late to go to the cinema.*
  a) She didn't have to go and see a film.
  b) She couldn't go and see a film.

5 *She had a lot of food in the fridge.*
  a) She didn't have to buy any food.
  b) She couldn't buy any food.

6 *Her flat was extremely clean and tidy.*
  a) She didn't have to clean it.
  b) She couldn't clean it.

2 Rewrite the sentences so that they refer to past time.

Example
All men must do two years' military service.
All men had to do two years' military service.

a) People can choose between the army and the navy.

_____

_____

b) All new soldiers must have a medical examination.

_____

_____

c) You can't join the army if you have a physical handicap.

_____

_____

d) You mustn't have long hair in the army.

_____

_____

e) Women don't have to do military service.

_____

_____

f) Foreigners don't have to register for military service.

_____

_____

Are any of these past or present sentences true for your country?

3 For each question, finish the second sentence so that it means the same as the first.

Example
Smoking is not allowed in the museum.
You mustn't smoke in the museum.

a) We spent two hours waiting in the queue.
We had _____

_____ .

b) It's a good idea to arrive at the museum early in the morning.
You _____

_____ .

c) It wasn't necessary to get a guide.
We didn't _____

_____ .

d) I don't think it's a good idea to go there with young children.
You _____

_____ .

e) You can visit the museum without paying on Wednesdays.
On Wednesdays, you don't _____

_____ .

f) They didn't let us take any photos.
We _____

_____ .

Listening

1 ▭ Cover the tapescript opposite and listen to a conversation between two men. Are the following sentences true or false?

a) Patrick went to a football match last night.

b) Patrick often talks to his wife about football.

c) Patrick doesn't know how to make his wife happy.

d) Brian thinks he understands women.

e) Brian has a good relationship with his wife.

2 ▭ Brian gives Patrick advice about women. Listen again and tick (✓) the pieces of advice that you hear.

Examples
Talk to your wife about football.
Work fifteen hours a day.

a) Don't give your wife any money.

b) Never do any housework.

c) Don't forget your wife's birthday.

d) Buy flowers for your wife.

e) Tell your wife that her hair looks nice.

f) Tell your wife to go on a diet.

g) Be nice to your wife's friends.

h) Don't complain about the telephone bills.

Brian Where were you last night, Patrick? You missed a really great match.

Patrick Oh, I had to baby-sit.

Brian Baby-sit?

Patrick Yeah, Julie went out with her friends.

Brian Did you tell her it was an important match?

Patrick No, of course not. You can't speak to women about football – they just don't understand things like that.

Brian No, no, you're right, Pat.

Patrick Actually, I don't think I understand women at all. Julie always seems to be fed up with me – I just don't know what I should do to make her happy.

Brian Oh, that's easy. You just have to work fifteen hours a day and give her all your money.

Patrick I do that anyway. And it's still not enough. Things were much easier for our dads. They didn't have to do any housework or cooking or shopping. I mean, I do loads of housework and she *still* isn't happy.

Brian Oh no, you mustn't do that! Women love complaining, and you have to give her something to complain about. I never do any housework.

Patrick Hey, Brian, what about equality and all that?

Brian Look, you don't have to do the housework to keep a woman happy. You just have to follow a few simple rules.

Patrick And what are these simple rules?

Brian Well, first of all, you mustn't forget her birthday or your wedding anniversary. Buy flowers and take her out for a nice meal.

Patrick Right. Anything else?

Brian You must notice her hair – tell her it looks nice. Oh, and ask her if she's lost weight. They love that.

Patrick Ha ha – yes, Julie's always on a diet.

Brian Hang on – that's not all. You must be nice to her friends – but not too nice. And – this is a big one – you mustn't complain about the phone bills.

Patrick Ha ha. Very good! I suppose you have the perfect marriage!

Brian Er no, actually. Sharon left me three weeks ago.

Vocabulary

1 Match the adjectives in the box to the descriptions below.

> cheerful   insecure   lazy   optimistic
> sensible   sensitive   silly   ~~talkative~~

Example

He never stops talking! *talkative*

a) She always thinks so carefully about everything she does!
b) She never wants to do any work!
c) He really understands other people and knows how to talk to them!
d) She thinks that everything will be fine!
e) He's always smiling and so happy!
f) She's got no confidence in herself at all!
g) He's like a child – more like five years old than twenty-five!

2 Circle the best alternative.

Example

A lot of people borrow money to pay for their university *career* / *studies* / *training*.

a) *Nursery* / *Primary* / *Secondary* schools are for children aged five to eleven.
b) Why do so many school children want to sit at the back of the *class* / *lecture* / *lesson*?
c) *Programmes* / *Subjects* / *Syllabuses* like Music and Art are often very popular.
d) Everybody in England *fails* / *passes* / *takes* exams called GCSEs when they are sixteen.
e) School *lecturers* / *professors* / *teachers* are not very well paid in the U.K.
f) Students get their *marks* / *notes* / *numbers* for their school-leaving exams at the end of the summer.
g) Many university *pupils* / *students* / *trainees* in England live in accommodation on the campus.

3 Complete each sentence with a preposition from the box.

> about   for   for   in   of   on
> ~~to~~   to   with

Example

According __to__ The Rules, you must never ask a man out.

a) You mustn't be too honest _____ your feelings.
b) I usually fall in love with men who are not good _____ me.
c) I disagree _____ The Rules.

d) Barbara had to say she was too busy to talk to Michael _____ the phone.
e) A boy from school invited me _____ his house.
f) Have you had enough _____ that cake or would you like some more?
g) Makiko's grandfather paid _____ her training.
h) They play an important role _____ preserving Japanese culture.

4 Match the book titles in box A to the subjects in box B. You will need to insert the missing vowels in box B.

A

> a) *An Idiot's Guide to Einstein's Relativity*
> b) *Banking and Finance Today*
> c) *Great Rivers of the World*
> d) *Pi – the Magic Number*
> e) *The Molecular Structure of Carbon*
> f) *The Sex Life of Giant Pandas*
> g) *Was Napoleon Murdered?*

B

> 1 B _ _ l _ gy
> 2 Ch _ m _ stry
> 3 _ c _ n _ m _ cs
> 4 G _ _ gr _ phy
> 5 H _ st _ ry
> 6 M _ ths
> 7 Phys _ cs

5 Complete each sentence with an appropriate form of the word in brackets.

Example

Stop looking so <u>miserable</u> (misery)!

a) Follow my _____ (advise) and you won't have any problems.
b) The train arrives at _____ (exact) nine o'clock.
c) People in big cities are not always very _____ (friend).
d) Every summer during my _____ (child), we went on holiday to Blackpool.
e) It was one of the most _____ (embarrass) experiences of my life.
f) Her parents didn't want her to marry a _____ (foreign).
g) She wore a _____ (tradition) white dress to the wedding.

Writing

1 Read the letter and replace the underlined phrases 1–10 with a phrase from the list below (a–j).

Dear Nicky,

(1) <u>Thanks so much for writing.</u> (2) <u>It was good to hear your news.</u> (3) <u>I'm sorry I haven't written for so long</u>, but (4) <u>I've been really busy.</u>

My big news is that I've split up with Michael. At first, I was really sad, but I feel much better about it now. I met a really nice guy the other day, but I don't think I'm ready for another boyfriend right now. I've got so much work to do that I haven't got the time!

Anyway, (5) <u>that's all the news for now</u>, but (6) <u>I promise I'll write again soon.</u> (7) <u>I must stop now to catch the post.</u> By the way, Doris (8) <u>sends her love.</u> (9) <u>Take care and write back soon.</u>

(10) <u>All the best,</u>
Barbara

a) asked me to say 'hi' ☐
b) Best wishes ☐
c) I have to go ☐
d) I'll be in touch soon ☐
e) I've had so much to do ☐
f) I was really pleased to read your news ☐
g) Look after yourself and keep in touch ☐
h) Many thanks for your letter ☐ 1
i) Sorry it's been so long since I last wrote ☐
j) That's about it for the moment ☐

2 In informal writing, it is usual to use contractions. Circle all the different contractions in Barbara's letter. What are the uncontracted (full) forms?

contracted form	full form
I'm	I am
_____	_____
_____	_____
_____	_____
_____	_____
_____	_____

3 Imagine that you are Barbara's friend. Write a reply to her letter. In the second paragraph of your letter, tell her your own personal news.

Pronunciation

Underline all the negative verbs that you can contract in the song titles below.

Example
<u>Can not</u> be with you tonight *(can't)*

a) I could not live without your love
b) I must not think of her
c) It does not have to be this way
d) Love does not have to hurt
e) She does not have to try
f) We really should not be doing this
g) You can not hurry love
h) You did not have to be so nice
i) You did not have to go
j) You do not have to say you love me
k) You do not have to worry

🔊 Repeat the song titles with the contracted verbs after the recording.

Grammar

1 Look at the sign in each question and choose the best explanation.

1

LEAVE KEYS AT RECEPTION

a) You couldn't leave your keys at reception.
b) You don't have to take your keys out of the hotel.
c) You didn't have to leave your keys at reception.
d) You must not take your keys out of the hotel.

2

Everything must go!

a) They have already sold everything.
b) They want to sell everything.
c) Everybody is going to leave.
d) They aren't going anywhere.

3

CLOSED
ALL ENQUIRIES TO OUR NEW SHOP AT
27, THE HIGH STREET

a) The shop is moving to a new building soon.
b) The new shop is going to close soon.
c) The shop has moved to a new building recently.
d) The new shop is not going to accept enquiries.

4

MAXIMUM WEIGHT
90 KILOS

a) Only put things here that are lighter than 90 kilos.
b) Don't put things here if they don't weigh as much as 90 kilos.
c) The lightest weight that you can put here is 90 kilos.
d) Put things here if they are heavier than 90 kilos.

5

BUY NOW, PAY LATER 0% INTEREST

a) You can pay the interest if you buy now.
b) You don't have to spend any money until later.
c) You mustn't pay any interest if you buy later.
d) You shouldn't buy anything now.

6

Castle Pizzeria
BEST PRICES IN TOWN

a) Pizzas are not as cheap here as in other pizzerias.
b) Other pizzerias are not as expensive as here.
c) You can buy the most expensive pizzas here.
d) Pizzas are more expensive in other pizzerias.

2 Each sentence has one word which should not be there. Cross it out.

Example
Could you explain ~~me~~ how to send an email?

a) Did you to have to wear a uniform at school?
b) Have you been go to the cinema recently?
c) I couldn't to invite my friends to my house.
d) I don't bother to going into supermarkets any more.
e) I'm not definitely not going to forget my real friends.
f) Matt is having eat lunch with Madonna and Guy on Monday.
g) My husband bought to me a silver bracelet for my birthday.
h) She is not hardly ever at home in the evenings.
i) I was wrote an angry letter to the bank yesterday.
j) There shouldn't to be different rules for men and women.
k) We were studied this with our teacher last year.

3 Rewrite the sentences beginning with the words given.

Example
We're not allowed to talk English in our German classes.
We must *not talk English in our German classes.*

a) Last week, my brother borrowed 20 euros from me.
Last week, I _____
_____

b) Unfortunately, it wasn't possible for me to finish the exercise.
Unfortunately, I _____
_____

c) I learnt French from my mother.
My mother _____
_____

d) It wasn't necessary for us to take the car.
We did _____
_____

e) She rarely arrives on time.
She hardly _____
_____

f) What are your plans for the weekend?
What are you _____
_____

g) I bought a cheap watch from a man in the street.
A man in the street _____
_____

h) I think it's a good idea for you to call him.
I think you _____
_____

i) You can get into the museum without paying after five o'clock.
You don't _____
_____

4 Complete the story by filling each gap with one word only.

We live in a very quiet village. We _hardly_ ever have any visitors, and many of the villagers have never been further (a) _____ the nearest town. But the older villagers have (b) _____ forgotten about the day that Princess Caraboo came to town. My grandmother (c) _____ me the story.

When the Princess arrived in the village, nobody (d) _____ understand her, because she spoke a very strange language. But the villagers did (e) _____ have to wait long because, a few days later, a Portuguese sailor also arrived. 'I (f) _____ been to her country,' he said. 'I will tell (g) _____ what she is saying. She comes from the island of Javasu and pirates brought (h) _____ here. Now, she is hoping to stay here to find peace.'

She made many friends and the owner of the local castle said, 'She is a princess and we (i) _____ look after her. She can stay with me and she will not have (j) _____ worry about money.'

For a long time, everybody was happy. Then, one day, a journalist showed a newspaper story and a photo to the castle owner. The photo looked just (k) _____ Princess Caraboo.
'Yes,' she admitted, 'it is me. But believe me, I (l) _____ never done anything like this before. My father is a poor man from another town. He dressed me in these clothes and he brought (m) _____ here to look for my fortune. My brother had to pretend to be a sailor.'
'I will never (n) _____ anyone your secret,' replied the castle owner. 'And I love (o) _____ with a princess. Will you marry me?'

Suddenly I realised that my grandmother was talking about herself. My grandfather kept his word and I am the only person that my grandmother has (p) _____ told.

Vocabulary

1 Choose the best alternative from the options below to fill the gaps.

At the St Louis Olympic Games of 1904, it was a hot, <u>humid</u> day and there were thirty-two starters in the (a) _____ race. Most of the (b) _____ had to (c) _____ before the end, but fourteen of them made it to the finish. One of them was a New Yorker, Fred Lorz.

Fred started feeling ill during the race, but (d) _____ for him a car stopped and gave him a (e) _____ . As he walked into the (f) _____ , people thought he was the (g) _____ . His (h) _____ was taken with the daughter of the President and they were going to give him the (i) _____ . But just then, someone (j) _____ that Fred hadn't bothered running the whole race – he had covered eleven miles as a passenger in a car. When the crowd (k) _____ that Fred had (l) _____ his victory in this (m) _____ way, they became (n) _____ and angry. Lorz had trouble leaving the stadium and he was not (o) _____ to run again for a long time.

Example

(humid)   rather   warm

a) athletics   human   marathon
b) careers   divers   runners
c) break down   come up   give up
d) fortunately   recently   silly
e) delivery   lift   speech
f) neighbourhood   stadium   studio
g) challenge   winner   vet
h) photograph   photographer   photography
i) gold medal   running water   solo career
j) found out   gave away   moved out
k) disagreed   realised   suggested
l) achieved   employed   respected
m) dishonest   insecure   sensible
n) decent   delighted   noisy
o) awarded   allowed   applied

2 Complete the story with words from the box. You can use the words more than once.

about	at	for	in	into	of	on
over	to	up				

Two men were sitting in a pub talking _about_ their sons.

'My son was no good (a) _____ his school work at all,' said the first man. 'He was only interested (b) _____ music. He was mad (c) _____ it. He joined a band and his first song went straight (d) _____ the top (e) _____ the charts. He's got plenty (f) _____ money now and he doesn't know what to spend it (g) _____ . Just last week, he bought a new house (h) _____ his best friend!'

'Ah,' said the second man. 'I was worried (i) _____ my son, too. He dropped out (j) _____ school because he thought it was a waste (k) _____ time. But then he applied (l) _____ a job in a bank and (m) _____ the years he's been really successful. (n) _____ fact, he's so rich now that he has just given his best friend a million pounds.' Just then, a third friend walked into the pub. 'What does your son do (o) _____ a living?' they asked.

'My son? I'll tell you (p) _____ my son,' said the third man. 'He's a lazy good-for-nothing. He's had one or two jobs, but he always gets tired (q) _____ them after a week or two and gives them (r) _____ . But he's got rich friends and he always seems to have loads (s) _____ money. He's just moved (t) _____ a new house that one friend gave him, and another friend has given him a million pounds!'

3 Complete each sentence by making an adjective from the word in brackets.

Example
He's a <u>dangerous</u> (danger) driver who always breaks the speed limit.

a) He was much more _____ (confidence) after doing the training course.

b) Is it better to be rich or _____ (fame)?

c) The waitress was very _____ (friend) and we left a good tip.

d) She tried to give up chocolate, but it only made her _____ (misery).

e) On a first date, you must be quiet and _____ (mystery).

f) Working in the maternity department of a large hospital is a very _____ (stress) job.

g) The Beatles were one of the most _____ (success) bands of all time.

h) I was invited to a _____ (tradition) Japanese tea ceremony.

---

4 Complete the crossword. You have seen all the words that you need in Units 1–9 of *Inside Out*. Some of the letters have been given to you.

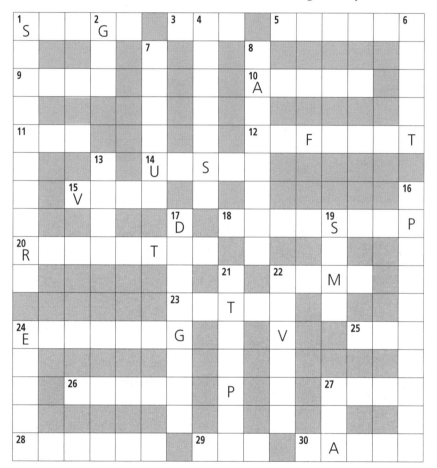

Clues

Across
1 place for actors in a theatre (5)
3 frozen water (3)
5 see picture 5 (6)
9 see picture 9 (4)
10 CD/record with lots of songs (5)
11 not dry (3)
12 to begin with (2,5)
14 angry/unhappy (5)
15 take part in an election (4)
18 place to buy books (8)
20 connected with love (8)
22 the military (4)
23 behaved (5)
24 making money (7)
25 opposite of *near* (3)
26 not dead (5)
27 opposite of *fat* (4)
28 see picture 28 (6)
29 put numbers together (3)
30 spend (money or time) badly (5)

Down
1 see picture 1 (10)
2 pop concert (3)
4 from China (7)
6 country in north Africa (5)
7 see picture 7 (6)
8 very long race (8)
13 see picture 13 (4)
16 what a person looks like (10)
17 not agree (8)
19 calculations (4)
21 with lines like a zebra (7)
22 suggestions/ recommendations (6)
24 the same (5)
27 British national drink (3)

11 *Smile*

Grammar

1 Test your knowledge of social customs around the world. Add *always* or *never* to the sentences.

Examples
Stop at a red light.   ***Always*** *stop at a red light.*
Drink and drive.   ***Never*** *drink and drive.*

a) Call the waiter 'garçon' in a French café.

b) Cross your knife and fork after a meal in Italy.

c) Eat with your left hand in north Africa.

d) Give a tip to New York taxi drivers.

e) Give money to the woman sitting outside Belgian toilets.

f) Say 'good morning' to people in English hotels at breakfast time.

g) Take off your shoes when you go into a Japanese house.

h) Kiss your colleagues at business meetings in China.

2 Look at the example. Some phrasal verbs do not take a direct object. Cross out the words in *italics* that should not be there. Four sentences are correct.

Example
Can you hold on ~~the telephone~~ and I'll get a pen?

a) I ran after *the bus* but unfortunately I missed it.

b) I think I'll stay up *the evening* and watch the late-night movie on TV.

c) I think it's better to deal with *the problem* now.

d) Switch off *the light* before you go out.

e) Why don't you sit down *the chair* and have a rest?

f) They decided to split up *their relationship* after three years together.

g) They called off *the wedding* because her father was ill.

3 Rewrite the phrases in *italics*, inserting the pronoun in brackets in the correct place.

Example
A: Two strawberry ice creams, please.
B: Strawberry? I'm sorry, *we've completely run out of.* (it)
   we've completely run out of it

a) A: What size is this, please?
   B: It's a size 46, madam. *Would you like to try on?* (it)
   _____

b) A: Is it serious?
   B: No, just stay in bed for a few days and *you'll soon get over.* (it)
   _____

c) A: We'll be happy to change your trousers if you show us the receipt.
   B: Oh dear, *I think I've thrown away!* (it)
   _____

d) A: You're just like your mother – *you really take after!* (her)
   B: And you're like your mother, too – bossy and selfish!
   _____

e) A: Is everything all right with your meal, sir?
   B: Yes, fine, but the music is very loud – *could you turn down, please?* (it)
   _____

f) A: You're not going out in that old coat, are you?
   B: Why not? I like it. *I'm not going to take off* just because you don't like it. (it)
   _____

g) A: Yes, I smoke a little, but only about thirty a day.
   B: Thirty cigarettes a day! *You must give up immediately!* (them)
   _____

Reading

1 Read the article about the Mona Lisa and match the paragraph titles to the paragraphs.

a) Is the Mona Lisa a copy? (*paragraph 3 *)
b) Who really was the Mona Lisa? (*paragraph ___*)
c) The birth of a painting (*paragraph ___*)
d) The French connection (*paragraph ___*)
e) The secret of the smile (*paragraph ___*)

2 Read the article again and decide if the following sentences are true (T) or false (F)?

a) Leonardo painted the Mona Lisa about five hundred years ago. ☐
b) He painted it very quickly. ☐
c) The Mona Lisa is a portrait of Vasari's wife. ☐
d) Louis XIV put the painting in the palace at Fontanebleau. ☐
e) The Louvre has not always been a museum. ☐
f) The thief wrote a letter to an American gallery. ☐
g) The Mona Lisa is possibly a self-portrait of Leonardo. ☐
h) You can't see the Mona Lisa's mouth very well. ☐

3 Look at the pronouns in *italics* in the article. What do they refer to?

Example
her (line 6)   *the Mona Lisa*

a) it (line (12) _____
b) him (line 14) _____
c) it (line 20) _____
d) it (line 22) _____
e) she (line 41) _____
f) they (line 46) _____

The Mona Lisa

The world's most famous smile – and the world's most famous painting – is Leonardo's Mona Lisa (La
5 *Gioconda). But how much do you know about **her**? Who is the mysterious woman and why is her smile so special?*

10 **1** Leonardo began work on this portrait around 1500 and spent many years working on **it**. According to the art historian Vasari, it is the portrait of the young wife of a merchant from Florence, but Leonardo never gave **him**
15 the picture. He kept it for himself.

2 Later the French king bought it and put it in the royal palace at Fontainebleau. Centuries later, the French king Louis XIV moved the palace to Versailles and the painting moved
20 too. For a while, Napoleon had **it** in his bedroom, but the Mona Lisa moved to the Louvre when **it** became a museum. It has not moved since then, apart from a few years at the beginning of the twentieth century.

25 **3** In 1911, the painting was stolen. It could not be found anywhere, but in 1913 the thief sent a letter to a gallery in Italy. He wanted to sell it. But why did the thief wait two years before returning it? During this time, many
30 copies of the painting were made and sold to American collectors. Is the painting now in the Louvre also a fake? Many people think that this is a real possibility.

4 Leonardo's painting is extremely life-like,
35 but many experts are not sure that it is a portrait of the woman from Florence. There are many theories, but perhaps the most interesting is that it is a portrait of Leonardo himself. An American expert has compared
40 Leonardo's self-portrait and the Mona Lisa and **she** has found that many of the features are exactly the same.

5 The two most important features of a face are the corners of the eyes and the mouth. If
45 you look at the painting, you will see that these features are blurred – **they** are much less clear than the rest of the face. As a result, the viewer has to imagine what the Mona Lisa is thinking. The mystery of her smile is just a
50 bit of clever artistic technique.

Vocabulary

1 Put the following parts of the face in order. Begin with the top of the face and end with the facial feature at the bottom of the face.

> cheek   ~~chin~~   eyebrow   eyelash
> ~~forehead~~   lip   moustache   teeth

<u>forehead</u>   d) _____

a) _____   e) _____

b) _____   f) _____

c) _____   <u>chin</u>

2 Read the character description for your astrological sign. Do you agree with it?

NUMEROLOGICAL *Astrology*

Add the four numbers of the year of your birth together, e.g. 1972 1+9+7+2 = 19
Find the Numerological Astrological sign that corresponds to you.

Earth 0–15

You are a hard-working, sensible realist. You are a loyal friend, but you are also ambitious at work. You are a little shy but you enjoy being with other people, who like your sense of humour.

Air 16–20

You are an easy-going sort of person – sociable and good fun to be with. You like to have a laugh and you are confident in most social situations. You are not always very sensitive and some people may think you are selfish.

Fire 21–24

You have a very warm personality, sometimes too warm, and some of your relationships are very stormy. At times, you are miserable and look for arguments with your friends or partner. You don't like bossy people and you don't like being in crowds.

Water 25–30

You are a secretive person and you may appear mysterious to people who do not know you well. You do not have enemies and you have a natural authority, but you find it hard to talk about yourself. You appear strong, although you are not always very sure of yourself.

3 Look in the text in exercise 2 to find adjectives for the following nouns.

noun	*adjective*
ambition	<u>ambitious</u>
a) confidence	_____
b) loyalty	_____
c) misery	_____
d) mystery	_____
e) secret	_____
f) strength	_____
g) warmth	_____

4 Cross out the noun phrases on the right that **cannot** be used with the phrasal verbs on the left.

Example
call off   *a meeting / a party / ~~a problem~~*

a) fill in   *an application / a form / a mess*
b) get over   *an illness / a problem / money*
c) give up   *music lessons / smoking / a coat*
d) put on   *a form / some music / your shoes*
e) switch on   *a computer / smoking / the TV*
f) take off   *your clothes / a test / your watch*
g) turn up   *a job / the music / the volume*

5 Complete each sentence with a particle from the box.

> after   away   away   down   off   ~~up~~
> up   with

Example
Don't leave your coat on the floor – hang it <u>up</u> .

a) Just sit _____ and relax – everything will be all right in a minute.
b) The teacher told the students to put their books _____ and get ready for the test.
c) They asked me to look _____ their flat while they were on holiday.
d) They switched _____ the TV and finally went to bed.
e) This room is real mess – clear it _____ immediately!
f) We really haven't got time to deal _____ that problem right now.
g) Why don't you throw _____ those old shoes and get some new ones?

Writing

1 Look at the three invitations below. For each invitation, underline the information you need to answer these questions.

- Who is the invitation from?
- What is the invitation for?
- When is the event?

Colonel and Mrs R. Peacock

❦

Request the pleasure of the company of

Roger & Tania Hunt

at the wedding of their daughter, Rosemary,
to Mr Jeremy Strutt on April 1st at 11.00
at St Margaret's Church, Rottingdean, Sussex
RSVP

WILD GANGSTERS PARTY
JOIN DAVID AND GAVIN TO SEE
IN THE NEW YEAR

DECEMBER 31 (FROM 9 P.M.)
BRING A BOTTLE (OR TWO)

P.S. WE'VE GOT PLENTY OF SPARE
ROOMS IF YOU NEED TO STAY THE
NIGHT. PLEASE LET US KNOW IF
YOU'RE PLANNING TO COME.
THE OLD BARN, UPPER TRIPPINGTON,
DEVON

Brenda,
The office is holding the annual Christmas party on December 21st this year. They've hired the Ministry of Dance and they've got a really good DJ. It would be great if you could come. Ask Mehmet to look after the baby – he hates dancing anyway.
Let me know before the end of the week if you're coming.

Love
Helen

P.S. Why don't you get your answering machine fixed?!

---

2 Look at two replies to the invitations. Some sentences are missing. Find the places (1–6) where the missing sentences (a–f) belong.

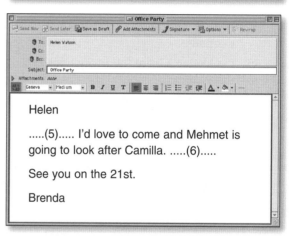

Dear Colonel and Mrs Peacock

.....(1)..... Unfortunately, Roger and I will be in Argentina at the beginning of April, so I'm afraid we won't be able to make it. .....(2).....

Please pass on our best wishes to the happy couple. .....(3).....

.....(4).....

Tania Hunt

Helen

.....(5)..... I'd love to come and Mehmet is going to look after Camilla. .....(6).....

See you on the 21st.

Brenda

---

a) I hope that everything goes well.
b) I'm writing to thank you for the invitation to Rosemary's wedding.
c) Thanks for the email.
d) We'll be in touch when we get back
e) I'm really looking forward to it.
f) Yours sincerely

3 Now write a reply to David and Gavin's invitation.

Pronunciation

Listen to the tongue twisters below and practise saying them.

What noise annoys an oyster most?
A noisy noise annoys an oyster most.
Busy buzzing bumble bees.

---

12 Rebel

Grammar

1 Four of the sentences below contain a grammatical mistake. Correct the sentences that are wrong.

Example

~~Are you having~~ internet access in your home? (Do you have)
They were having a party when we arrived. ✓

a) He is having a poster of Anna Kournikova on his bedroom wall.

b) How many countries are having nuclear weapons?

c) I'm having a lot of fun in my English classes this year.

d) When she's having breakfast, she likes to read the newspaper.

e) She was having a boyfriend who worked in a circus last year.

f) She was having a relationship with an older man when I last saw her.

g) She was having some difficulties with the exercise until I helped her.

h) She is having pink hair and a ring in her nose.

2 Circle the correct verb form.

James Dean (only made) / was only made three films in his short life but he (a) *remains / is remained* a legend of the cinema. He (b) *knows best / is best known* for his role in 'Rebel Without A Cause' where he (c) *plays / is played* the part of a rebellious teenager.

Dean was born in 1931. His mother (d) *died / was died* when he was young and he (e) *brought up / was brought up* by his aunt and uncle. After high school, he (f) *went / was gone* to California, where he (g) *gave / was given* a place at the Actors'

Studio, a famous acting school. After a few jobs in TV dramas, he (h) *saw / was seen* by Warner Brothers and (i) *gave / was given* his first film role, in 'East Of Eden'. He (j) *became / was become* a star almost immediately, but it was the beginning of a very short career. In 1955, at the age of 24, he (k) *killed / was killed* in a car crash.

3 Put the verbs in brackets into the past simple tense. In each sentence, one verb is active and the other is passive.

Example
In 1955, Che Guevara _joined_ (join) Fidel Castro's Cuban rebels in Mexico and he _was trained_ (train) as a soldier.

a) A year later, the rebels _____ (land) in Cuba and Che _____ (name) commander of the army.

b) The following year, the Cuban dictator, Batista, _____ (defeat) and Castro _____ (become) president.

c) After the revolution, Che's first book _____ (publish) and he _____ (become) a minister in the government.

d) For a few years, he _____ (travel) to many different countries where he _____ (welcome) by socialist heads of state.

e) In 1965, he _____ (join) a guerrilla army in the Congo but they _____ (defeat) by government soldiers.

f) Two years later in Bolivia, his guerrilla army _____ (win) two battles against the government, but his friend, Régis Debray, _____ (catch).

g) A month later, the guerrillas _____ (fight) the Bolivian army again and Che _____ (kill).

h) The news _____ (announce) the next day but many people _____ (not believe) it until much later.

Listening and reading

1 🔲 Cover the tapescript opposite and listen to a radio interview. Match it to one of the newspaper cuttings below.

Anti-globalisation leader arrested

The well-known Dutch activist, Sandra Van Praag has been arrested following a violent demonstration outside a McDonald's in Strasbourg. Van Praag was held overnight and will appear in court later today. In a statement to the press, a lawyer for Ms Van Praag said that she had been charged with violent

Peaceful demonstration turns violent

It is believed that as many as 70 anti-globalisation protesters have been arrested in Strasbourg following violent clashes with the police. The demonstration outside the European Parliament began peacefully but fighting broke out when protesters set fire to a car in front of the parliament building. A police

2 🔲 Listen again and complete each sentence with a past participle.

Example
Nine police officers were _injured_.

a) Two million euros of damage was _____ to shops and cars.

b) Permission was not _____ for the march.

c) Many people were _____ in the French and American revolutions.

d) Cars were _____ on fire.

e) A McDonald's was _____ by French activists.

f) Four French activists were _____ to prison.

3 Put the following words and phrases in the appropriate places in the tapescript. The first one has been done for you.

a fairer system	a group	anti-police
a peaceful protest	our cause	the law
~~the organisers~~	demonstrators	leaflets

Presenter Our guest today is Sandra Van Praag, one of _the organisers_ of the demonstration that took place in Strasbourg yesterday. Sandra – seventy-four (a) _____ were arrested, nine police officers were injured and over two million euros of damage was done to shops and cars. Is the violence necessary?

Sandra I think that the violence is unfortunate. The demonstration began as (b) _____ march. We were handing out (c) _____ outside the European parliament and the police wanted to stop us. There was a happy, party atmosphere until the police began arresting people.

Presenter But permission was not given for the march. The government said no. The police were just doing their job, weren't they?

Sandra We're not (d) _____, but sometimes it is necessary to break the law if you really care about your cause. Look at the French Revolution, look at the American Revolution. Think about Nelson Mandela. There was fighting, there was violence, many people were killed, but afterwards there was (e) _____.

Presenter In other words, you encourage people to break (f) _____?

Sandra It is true that cars were set on fire, but I do not support the people who did this. I am against the people who throw stones at the police. Much of this violence is just stupid, young people having what they call fun. But sometimes, yes. A few years ago, a McDonald's was attacked by (g) _____ of French activists. They took it to pieces. Four of them were sent to prison, but their action was important – and successful. Since that time, people have started talking a lot more about...

Presenter And was your march yesterday successful?

Sandra I think that 30,000 people is a success, yes. (h) _____ has received a lot of publicity and...

Presenter Sandra, I'm afraid we've run out of time there. Thank you for joining us on the programme. And now...

Vocabulary

1 Complete the text with words from the box.

about	against	at	away	in	into
~~of~~	of	out	to	with	

I became a member _of_ ATTAC because I care
(a) _____ the situation in some countries that
have got (b) _____ serious debt. I'm (c) _____
the globalisation of the world economy and I
decided to take part (d) _____ the
demonstration. The members of ATTAC are
supporters (e) _____ peaceful action and we
disagree (f) _____ violence. Unfortunately, some
demonstrators broke (g) _____ from the march
and violence broke (h) _____ . They started
throwing stones (i) _____ the police and they
even set fire (j) _____ a car in the street.

2 Combine a word from box A with a word from
box B to make compound nouns. Then use these
compound nouns to complete the sentences
below.

A

~~animal~~
bottle
foreign
fur
nuclear
plastic
protest
public
student

B

bags
banks
coats
fees
marches
ministers
~~testing~~
transport
weapons

Example
Some companies have stopped animal testing in
the development of beauty products.

a) European _____ are
   meeting later today to discuss the crisis in
   Afghanistan.
b) In England, the government used to pay for
   _____ but now you have
   to borrow the money.
c) Many people have stopped wearing
   _____ because they are
   against cruelty to animals.
d) Many places now have _____
   _____ and the broken glass is
   recycled.

e) Spending more money on _____
   _____ is a good way of reducing
   traffic pollution.
f) Supermarkets give away millions of
   _____ every day.
g) The last time that _____
   were used was in 1945.
h) There have been _____
   in Genoa, Brussels and Stockholm against
   globalisation.

3 Complete each sentence with the noun form of
the word in brackets.

Example
Everyone should have the right to a basic
education (educate).

a) 'Friends of the Earth' is an _____
   (organise) that cares about the environment.
b) Her _____ (fascinate) with the circus
   started at an early age.
c) In some countries, there is no _____
   (separate) of religion and politics.
d) Many British politicians support the
   _____ (legalise) of cannabis.
e) The government announced their
   _____ (decide) to ban smoking in
   public places.
f) There is an _____ (exhibit) of Russian
   revolutionary posters at the art gallery.
g) There was a _____ (reduce) in
   financial aid to third world countries last
   year.
h) They put up the Christmas _____
   (decorate) on December 1st.

4 Put the sentences in the correct order to complete
the story.
a) He was held prisoner for thirty days.
b) He was released.
c) His family paid the ransom.
d) The judge sent them to prison.
e) The kidnappers were pardoned by the
   president.
f) The police arrested the kidnappers.
g) The son of a businessman was kidnapped
   and his bodyguard was killed.
h) They were charged with kidnap and murder.

1	2	3	4	5	6	7	8
g							e

Writing

1 Look at the results of a survey that was carried out in Great Britain. A group of a hundred young adults was asked what they thought about the problems that they face today.

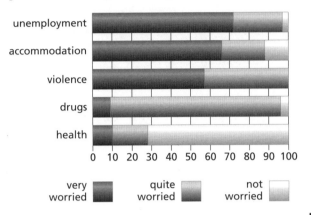

very worried quite worried not worried

Complete the report using words or phrases from the box.

a few   ~~everybody~~   large number
majority   most   nobody   none
several   small number

A survey was carried out in Great Britain to find out what young people are most worried about.

The results of the survey show that nearly _everybody_ thought that unemployment was the biggest problem facing them. Only a
(a) _____ of people were not worried about it at all.

(b) _____ people thought that accommodation was also a big problem, but
(c) _____ said they didn't worry about it.

A (d) _____ of people were worried about violence and
(e) _____ of the people interviewed said that it did not matter at all.

Only (f) _____ people were very worried about drugs, but almost
(g) _____ said this did not concern them at all. A few were also very worried about health, but the
(h) _____ were not concerned.

Perhaps, most importantly, the survey shows that a lot of young people today are worried about a lot of things.

2 The survey also asked people about what was important in their lives. Look at the chart and write a short report about this information. Use as many words and phrases from the box in exercise 1 as possible.

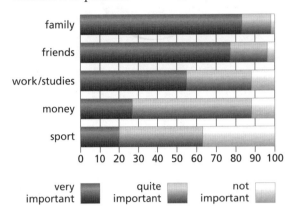

very important   quite important   not important

Pronunciation

Mark the main stress in the words in *italics*.

Everybody's talking about
Missions, ambitions, traditions and *permissions,*
Work *conditions, competitions.*
All we are saying is ...

Everybody's talking about
Associations, corporations, obligations
Accommodation applications, populations,
    destinations.
All we are saying is ...

Listen to the recording to check your answers.

13 Dance

Grammar

1 Complete the sentences with *for* or *since*.

Example
I've had a headache <u>since</u> I woke up.

a) I haven't been to a beach _____ last summer.

b) I haven't watched a football match _____ over a week.

c) I've had this book _____ a couple of months.

d) I haven't had a cup of coffee _____ early this morning.

e) I've known my best friend _____ we were very young.

f) I've lived in this town _____ three years.

g) I haven't seen my neighbour _____ the beginning of last week.

h) I've studied English _____ about a year and a half.

Now rewrite the sentences so that they are true for you.

2 Complete the sentences with *been* or *gone*.

Examples
Have you <u>been</u> abroad this year?
She's on the beach – she's <u>gone</u> for a swim.

a) He won't be long – he's just _____ to the bar.

b) He's never _____ to a nightclub.

c) I haven't _____ to a rock concert for ages.

d) I'm afraid she's _____ out for lunch – can I take a message?

e) I've _____ to the doctor but she told me not to worry.

f) She's _____ to the shops but she'll be back soon.

g) They've _____ to twelve different clubs since they arrived on the island.

h) Where's Wally? Has he _____ out somewhere?

3 Complete the second sentence so that it means the same as the first. Use an appropriate form of the verb in brackets.

Example
She started as a DJ two years ago.
She <u>has been a DJ for</u> two years. (be)

a) She became a fashion model in 1999.
She _____ 1999.
(be)

b) She started being famous when she appeared on TV.
She _____ she appeared on TV. (be)

c) They got married forty-nine years ago.
They _____
forty-nine years. (be)

d) He arrived in New York on Friday.
He _____ Friday.
(be)

e) I met him four years ago.
I _____ four years.
(know)

f) When did he get the tattoo?
How long _____
the tattoo? (have)

4 Put the verbs in brackets into the present perfect simple or the present perfect continuous.

Example
She <u>has known</u> (know) him since they were at school.

a) I _____ (be) a resident DJ for two years now.

b) I _____ (build) my own house, but it's not finished yet.

c) I _____ (save) money for my holiday and I only need another £50.

d) I'm knackered! I _____ (dance) all night.

e) Ibiza _____ (be) the clubbing capital of the world since the 1960s.

f) The club _____ (have) a roof for ten years.

Reading

1 Read the review of Billy Elliot and complete the cast list.

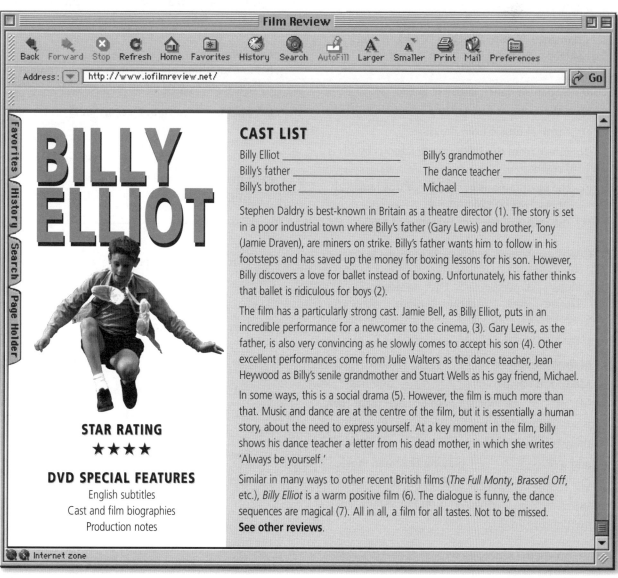

Film Review

Back Forward Stop Refresh Home Favorites History Search AutoFill Larger Smaller Print Mail Preferences

Address: http://www.iofilmreview.net/   Go

BILLY ELLIOT

STAR RATING
★★★★

DVD SPECIAL FEATURES
English subtitles
Cast and film biographies
Production notes

CAST LIST

Billy Elliot _____   Billy's grandmother _____
Billy's father _____   The dance teacher _____
Billy's brother _____   Michael _____

Stephen Daldry is best-known in Britain as a theatre director (1). The story is set in a poor industrial town where Billy's father (Gary Lewis) and brother, Tony (Jamie Draven), are miners on strike. Billy's father wants him to follow in his footsteps and has saved up the money for boxing lessons for his son. However, Billy discovers a love for ballet instead of boxing. Unfortunately, his father thinks that ballet is ridiculous for boys (2).

The film has a particularly strong cast. Jamie Bell, as Billy Elliot, puts in an incredible performance for a newcomer to the cinema, (3). Gary Lewis, as the father, is also very convincing as he slowly comes to accept his son (4). Other excellent performances come from Julie Walters as the dance teacher, Jean Heywood as Billy's senile grandmother and Stuart Wells as his gay friend, Michael.

In some ways, this is a social drama (5). However, the film is much more than that. Music and dance are at the centre of the film, but it is essentially a human story, about the need to express yourself. At a key moment in the film, Billy shows his dance teacher a letter from his dead mother, in which she writes 'Always be yourself.'

Similar in many ways to other recent British films (*The Full Monty*, *Brassed Off*, etc.), *Billy Elliot* is a warm positive film (6). The dialogue is funny, the dance sequences are magical (7). All in all, a film for all tastes. Not to be missed. **See other reviews**.

Internet zone

2 Find the places (1–7) in the review where the following phrases could be added.

a) and the whole experience is a celebration of humanity ☐

b) and this is his first full-length work for the cinema [1]

c) and his dancing is sensational ☐

d) and is less than pleased when he finds out about Billy's new interest ☐

e) and it leaves the audience feeling good as they come out of the cinema ☐

f) and we see the hardness of these working-class lives ☐

g) and finally helps him go to London for his dancing ☐

3 Tick (✓) the topics below which are mentioned in the review.

a) similar films   f) the photography
b) the acting   g) the dancing
c) the film studio   h) the price
d) the dialogue   i) the special effects
e) the director   j) the story

4 Find words or phrases in the review which mean the same as the following.

a) most famous (*paragraph 1*)

b) do the same as him (*paragraph 1*)

c) stupid (*paragraph 1*)

d) put your feelings into words or actions (*paragraph 3*)

e) an important time (*paragraph 3*)

f) that everybody will like (*paragraph 4*)

Vocabulary

1 Match the words in the box to the descriptions below.

> flamenco   pop   reggae   rock 'n' roll
> samba   waltz

a)   a Spanish dance to guitar music

b)   a three-step dance for two people

c)   carnival music from Brazil

d)   music from the 1950s, made famous by Elvis Presley

e)   the most famous performer of this Jamaican music was Bob Marley

f)   the music of the Top Twenty and MTV

2 Complete the text with words from the box.

> clubs   dance floors   DJ   ~~famous~~
> House   live   nightlife   room   stage

London is _famous_ for its (a) _____ and one of the best-known (b) _____ is Bar Madrid. It has two (c) _____ and has (d) _____ for 575 people. Each night there is something different. On Mondays, for example, there is a choice between (e) _____ bands and a (f) _____ playing Brazilian music. On Tuesdays, which is student night, they play (g) _____ music and on Thursdays, there are dancers on (h) _____ .

3 Complete the sentences with *at* or *on*.

Example
They first met _at_ a friend's wedding.

a)   He asked her to dance _____ the party after the wedding.

b)   They spent the whole afternoon _____ the dance floor.

c)   He spoke to her _____ the phone the next day.

d)   She invited him to a ballet _____ the opera house.

e)   Afterwards, they had dinner _____ a restaurant near the opera.

f)   The restaurant had a terrace _____ the roof.

g)   They sat talking _____ the terrace until the restaurant closed.

h)   After that, he took her to a disco _____ his football club.

4 Replace the words in *italics* with an informal word or phrase from the box.

> guy   knackered   laid-back   pretty
> reckon   ~~telly~~   winding him up

Example
Is there anything good on the *television* tonight?
Is there anything good on the telly tonight?

a)   His stamp collection is *quite* good.

_____

_____

b)   I met a really nice *man* on holiday last summer.

_____

_____

c)   I *think* she used to be a hippy.

_____

_____

d)   I was really *tired* after the party.

_____

_____

e)   She enjoyed *making him angry*.

_____

_____

f)   She has a *very relaxed* approach to life.

_____

_____

5 Complete each sentence with a preposition from the box.

> about   ~~at~~   for   for   of   on   to
> with

Example
Frank is very good _at_ Irish folk dancing.

a)   How worried are you _____ your image?

b)   How would you describe your attitude _____ dancing?

c)   Ibiza is famous _____ its night clubs.

d)   The club has space _____ 5,000 people.

e)   The film is based _____ a book by Stephen King.

f)   The swimming pool is the size _____ a football pitch.

g)   There's nothing wrong _____ ballet.

Writing

1 Look at the paragraph plan of a description of La Scala and put the paragraphs in the correct order.

1 Introduction and location: *paragraph* ___
2 General description: *paragraph* ___
3 Things to see and do: *paragraph* ___

MILAN'S FAMOUS
La Scala

a

It was built in the eighteenth century and has a beautiful façade. When you arrive, you go into a beautiful foyer with palm trees and huge mirrors. The interior of the theatre is decorated in red and gold and has room for over 200 people.

b

Apart from the operas, you can also see ballet and concerts of classical music. There is an interesting theatre museum and you can have guided tours of the theatre itself.

c

La Scala in Milan is one of the world's most famous opera houses. It is situated in the centre of the city, not far from the Cathedral.

2 Complete the sentences below with *because* or *because of*.

Examples
You need to book tickets in advance _because_ it is so popular.
La Scala closed for three years in 2002 _because of_ building work.

a) It was called La Scala _____ a church that used to be on the site.

b) The theatre was rebuilt in 1945 _____ it had been damaged during the Second World War.

c) Opera fans want to go there _____ it is the world's most famous theatre.

d) You can no longer stand at La Scala _____ fire regulations.

e) December is a good time to visit _____ there are many cultural events then.

f) It's not a good idea to drive there _____ the traffic problems in the centre of Milan.

3 Write a short description (approximately a hundred words) of an interesting building in your town or a building that you know. Use the article about La Scala and the paragraph plan to help you.

Pronunciation

1 🔲 Listen to the short pronunciation of *for* in the phrases below.

for ages   for two years   for a few days

What is the short pronunciation of the underlined words in the phrases below?

good at it   a lot of space   talk to me

Listen to the recording to check.

2 🔲 Listen and repeat the sentences below, paying attention to the short pronunciation of the underlined words.

a) What's your favourite place _for_ dancing?

b) Is your town famous _for_ its nightlife?

c) Do you prefer dancing _at_ a club or a party?

d) He pointed _at_ a chair.

e) What kinds _of_ music do they play?

f) It has a population _of_ 80,000.

g) I don't go _to_ pop concerts.

h) I haven't been _to_ the beach yet.

14 *Call*

Grammar

1 For each situation below, choose the best question.

1 Someone has got their bag on the seat of a bus. You want them to move it so that you can sit down. You say:

  a) Could you move your bag, please?
  b) Shall I move your bag, please?
  c) Would you like me to move your bag, please?

2 You see a person on the street outside your house. They look lost. You say:

  a) Could you show me the way?
  b) Would you mind showing me the way?
  c) Would you like me to show you the way?

3 You are in London near Big Ben. You would like someone to take your photo. You say:
  a) Is it okay if I take your photo?
  b) Shall I take your photo?
  c) Would you mind taking my photo, please?

4 A friend of yours says that she is feeling very ill. You say:

  a) I was wondering if you could call the doctor.
  b) Shall I call the doctor?
  c) Would you mind calling the doctor?

5 Your car has broken down. You stop a person in the street. You say:

  a) Could you possibly help me push the car?
  b) Is it okay if I push your car?
  c) Would you like me to push your car?

2 Rewrite the questions beginning with the words given.

Example
Does he love me?
Do you think *he loves me* ?

a) Will he return my call?

  Do you think _he_____

  _____ ?

b) What time is the meeting?

  Can you remember _____

  _____ ?

c) How much does a beer cost?

  Could you tell me _____

  _____ ?

d) Did he pass on the message?

  Do you know _____

  _____ ?

e) What does 'worried sick' mean?

  Do you know _____

  _____ ?

f) What do you think of my outfit?

  Could you tell me _____

  _____ ?

g) Who did you speak to?

  Can you remember _____

  _____ ?

3 Rearrange the words to make indirect questions.

Example
a any Have idea is what
you Zoomatron ?
Have you any idea what a Zoomatron is?

a) keys my I put Can remember car where you ?

  Can _____

  _____ ?

b) costs Do dollars how in know much this you ?

  Do _____

  _____ ?

c) Could is me tell the theatre where you ?

  Could _____

  _____ ?

d) against Do is it law the think you ?

  Do _____

  _____ ?

e) Do if is know married she you ?

  Do _____

  _____ ?

Listening

1   [cassette icon]   Cover the tapescript opposite and listen to three telephone conversations. Match the conversations to the 'phone moans' below.

a)   'I like to talk to a real person on the phone, but nowadays you get a recorded message which gives you all these options to choose from.'

b)   'I hate it when the person I'm speaking to starts drinking a cup of tea or eating something. It sounds disgusting!'

c)   'I hate it when you telephone a company or an office and you can never get through to the person you want to speak to.'

2   [cassette icon]   Listen to the conversations again. When you hear a phrase, write the number of the conversation next to it.

a)   Is ... there, please?   [1]

b)   Who's calling?   [ ]

c)   I'd like to speak to ...   [ ]

d)   Could I speak to ...?   [ ]

e)   Sorry, she's not in at the moment.   [ ]

f)   Thank you for calling.   [ ]

g)   I'll put you through.   [ ]

h)   Can you tell her I called, please?   [ ]

i)   Please hold.   [ ]

j)   You've got the wrong extension.   [ ]

k)   Can I take a message?   [ ]

l)   No one is available to take your call   [ ]

3   Write two short telephone conversations using some of the phrases in exercise 2.

Conversation 1
A: 677 3144.
B: Oh, hello. Is Satia there, please?
A: Er, just a moment. Who's calling?
B: It's Francesca. Is Satia in?
A: Er, sorry, she's not in at the moment.
B: Oh, right. Can you tell her I called, please?
A: Yeah, sure. Can I take a message?
B: No, no thanks. Just 'Francesca called', okay?
A: Okay. What did you say your name was?
B: Francesca. F-R-A-N-C-E-S-C-A.
A: Okay, I'll tell her. Bye.

Conversation 2
C: Oh, hello. I'd like to speak to someone ...
D: This is Goldcard Financial services. Thank you for calling. If you have a star button on your telephone, please press it twice now. If not, please hold ... Thank you. To report a stolen card, please press 'one'. For 'billing', please press 'two'. For all other services, please hold.
C: Oh, never mind.

Conversation 3
E: Good morning, XLCom. Can I help you?
F: Yes, good morning. Could I speak to someone in the technical support department, please?
E: Yes, of course. I'll put you through.
F: Thank you.
G: Dave here.
F: Oh, hello. Is that the technical support department?
G: Sorry. You've got the wrong extension. Hang on and I'll connect you.
H: Hello.
F: Oh, hello. Is that the technical support department?
H: Yes.
F: Could I speak to the manager, please?
H: Speaking.
F: Ah, well, I've got a problem with a new mobile phone –
H: Ah, you need another department. This is the business network division. Hold on, please, and I'll put you through.
I: I'm afraid no one is available to take your call right now. Please leave your name and telephone number after the beep and we'll...

Vocabulary

1 Complete the text with words from the box.

call	dialled	~~directory~~	extension
line	message	mobile	operator
voicemail			

I didn't have his number so I called _directory_ enquiries. The (a) _____ gave me his office number. I (b) _____ the number, but his (c) _____ was busy and I had to leave a (d) _____ on his (e) _____ . I asked him to return my (f) _____ . Then, I decided to try his (g) _____ . I got through, but there was a bad (h) _____ . When we finally spoke, I couldn't remember why I wanted to call him!

2 Complete the sentences with *said, told* or *asked*.

Example
I _asked_ my parents for a mobile phone for Christmas.

a) They _____ me that I was too young for a phone.
b) I _____ that I needed one.
c) They _____ it was too expensive.
d) I _____ for a pay-as-you-go phone.
e) I _____ them that it was very cheap.
f) My father _____ no.
g) My mother _____ me if I minded.
h) I _____ her it was okay.
i) I _____ I would ask my grandparents.

3 Complete the sentences with *at, in* or *on*.

Example
He's not _at_ his desk right now, I'm afraid.

a) Is it okay if I put you _____ hold?
b) Guess who I saw _____ the airport when I was waiting for a taxi?
c) The line's busy – he's probably _____ the Internet.
d) I probably won't be _____ home this evening.
e) What's that strange noise _____ the background?
f) Where _____ earth have you been?
g) Why can't they leave us _____ peace?

h) You can always call me _____ an emergency.
i) I'll meet you _____ the station, outside the main entrance, okay?
j) You've been _____ the phone for hours.

4 Complete each sentence with a verb from the box.

| come | get | give | hang | ~~look~~ | pass |
| pick | put | run | | | |

Example
Yes, you can borrow my phone, but you must _look_ after it.

a) Can you _____ on and I'll see if he's here?
b) Give me a call when you arrive and I'll come and _____ you up.
c) I asked the operator to _____ me through but I got cut off.
d) I'm going to keep leaving messages till he rings me back – I refuse to _____ up.
e) I want to get one of those new miniature phones that have just _____ out.
f) Send me an email if you can't _____ through.
g) This is going to be quick – I've almost _____ out of credit on my phone card.
h) Would you like me to _____ on a message?

5 Put the conversation in the correct order.

a) Erm... Could you take my number and ask someone to call me back?
b) Good afternoon. Sharecare Babysitting Services. Can I help you?
c) I'm afraid the booking secretary is busy right now. Would you mind holding?
d) Many thanks. Bye.
e) No problem, Mrs Blair. I'll pass on the message.
f) Of course, madam. Could I take your name?
g) Yes, good afternoon. I'd like to book a baby-sitter for this evening, please.
h) Yes, it's B-L-A-I-R, Blair. And the number is 0207 666 666.

1	2	3	4	5	6	7	8
b							d

Writing

1   Cover the tapescript and listen to telephone conversations 1–3. Complete the messages below.

1
Mr _____ from
_____ Bank called
– call him back:
020 768 _____

2
_____ called
– he's cancelled
_____ this evening.
Next _____ okay.

3
_____ from AWOL Travel
says your _____ for
Bangkok are ready.

2   Now listen to conversations 4 and 5 and take messages for each one.

Conversation 1
A: Hello.
B: Good afternoon. Could I speak to Mrs Walton, please?
A: I'm afraid she's not in. Can I help?
B: Er, I'm calling from Credit Bank. Could you tell me when she'll be back?
A: I'm not sure. Can I ask her to call you back?
B: That would be kind of you. My name's Sharma – that's S-H-A-R-M-A – from Credit Bank and the number is 020 768 9004.
A: Okay, Mr Sharma. I'll ask her to call you.
B: Thank you very much indeed.
A: You're welcome. Bye.

Conversation 2
A: Hello.
C: Oh, hi. Is that Dave? It's Richard here.
A: Hi, Richard. How are you?
C: Fine. And you?
A: Yeah, I'm all right.
C: Is Emma in?
A: No, she's gone out somewhere. I think she'll be back about six. Do you want me to take a message?
C: Yeah, I've got a lot of work at the office. Could you tell her that I can't play tennis this evening? I've already called the sports centre to cancel. Tell her I'm sorry but next week will be okay.

A: Okay, I'll tell her. But next week is okay, you said?
C: Yeah, next week is fine. Listen, I must run. I've got a million things to do.
A: Okay, speak to you soon. Bye.
C: See you.

Conversation 3
A: Hello.
D: Good afternoon. Could I speak to Mrs Walton, please?
A: She's not here right now. Can I help?
D: It's Mary here from AWOL Travel. She knows me. It's just to say that her tickets are ready.
A: Her tickets?
D: Yes, that's right. Her tickets for Bangkok. She can pick them up any time.
A: Tickets for Bangkok... Okay, I'll tell her. Many thanks.
D: Thanks. Bye.

Conversation 4
A: Hello.
E: Hello, Mrs Walton?
A: No, this is Dave Walton speaking.
E: Oh, right. Could I speak to Mrs Walton, please?
A: She's not in, I'm afraid.
E: Oh, I'm calling about her advertisement for a babysitter.
A: Well, I'm afraid she's not here at the moment.
E: Can I, er, can she call me back, please?
A: Sure.
E My name's Petra and my number is 0474 355899. Any time after 6 o'clock this evening.
A: Okay, Petra, I'll ask her. Thanks.
E: Thanks, Mr Walton. Bye.

Conversation 5
A: Hello.
F: Dave? Hi, it's Brenda here. Is Emma in?
A: No, she's at the supermarket, I think.
F Oh, right. Er, could you do me a favour?
A: Yeah, sure.
F: Well, could you tell her that we've got a meeting first thing tomorrow morning at eight o'clock? At the office. It's with somebody from the Tax Department, so it's really important that she's there.
A: Eight o'clock tomorrow? I'll tell her.
F: Thanks, Dave. I'll see you at the weekend, okay?
A: Yeah, see you then. Bye.

Review 3

Grammar

1 Put the words in the box into the three categories (*verbs, nouns* or *adjectives*) in column A. Then complete column B.

~~agree~~	~~bossy~~	carry	commit	deep
easy	enjoy	~~factory~~	good	illness
hide	hold	kidnap	knife	luxury
rob	roof	rude	run	silly	throw
toe	untidy	wide	wife	

A	**B**
verbs	*past participle*
agree	agreed
_____	_____
_____	_____
_____	_____
_____	_____
_____	_____
_____	_____
_____	_____
_____	_____

nouns	*plural*
factory	factories
_____	_____
_____	_____
_____	_____
_____	_____
_____	_____

adjectives	*superlative*
bossy	bossiest
_____	_____
_____	_____
_____	_____
_____	_____
_____	_____
_____	_____

2 Rearrange the words to make questions.

Example
any children got Have you ?
Have you got any children?

a) Do films James Bond like you ?

_____

_____

b) Are going of out thinking tonight you ?

_____

_____

c) abroad been Have this year you ?

_____

_____

d) been have here How living long you ?

_____

_____

e) been cinema Have recently the to you ?

_____

_____

f) help like me to Would you you ?

_____

_____

3 Each of the sentences below has *one* word missing. Insert the missing words.

Example   to
I'm looking forward∕going out tonight.

a) A Che poster pinned on his wall when he was a student.

b) How long you been studying English?

c) I been a DJ for two years.

d) I was wondering you could lend me your car.

e) Is okay if I bring my friend?

f) Rosie looking for a new place to live.

g) She kidnapped by a revolutionary group.

4 Circle the best alternative.

One day in a poor country, a man went to a bread shop to buy some bread. There was a long queue and he spoke to a woman (at) / on the front of the queue.

'Excuse me, how long (a) *have you been /* *you have been* here?'

'Oh, (b) *for / since* about four hours,' the woman replied. 'They (c) *said / told* us the shop would open soon.'

The man was in a hurry and decided to ask the woman (d) *help / to help* him. She (e) *looked / was looking* very friendly. 'Would you mind (f) *buying / to buy* a loaf of bread for me?' he asked politely.

'I'm afraid we're only (g) *allow / allowed* to buy one loaf each,' the woman replied.

This is crazy, (h) *thought / was thought* the man. What a country! He decided (i) *going / to go* to the presidential palace. He wanted to (j) *say / tell* the President what he (k) *thought him of / thought of him*. He got out his best suit, (l) *put it on / put on it* and walked to the palace.

Outside the palace, he (m) *asked / was asked* by a policeman what he wanted.

'I (n) *have been coming / have come* to speak to the President. Could you tell me where (o) *he is / is he*?'

'Certainly,' (p) *replied / was replied* the policeman. '(q) *Do join / Join* the queue over there. But I must warn you – the people (r) *at / on* the front (s) *have been waited / have been waiting* (t) *for / since* weeks.'

5 Rewrite the sentences beginning with the words given.

Example
Have you got any children?
Do you *have any children?*

a) She told me not to be late.
She said to me, '_____

_____

b) President Clinton pardoned her in 2001.
She was _____

_____

c) The photo of Che was taken by Alexander Korda.
Alexander Korda _____

_____

d) The last time I went to the cinema was a month ago.
I haven't _____

_____

e) Saskia started as a DJ two years ago.
Saskia has _____

_____

f) Shall I call you later?
Would you _____

_____

g) Could you take a message?
I was wondering if _____

_____

6 Find a response in box B to the sentences in box A.

A

a) Are you having a good time?
b) Come on. Hurry up!
c) Do you have any idea how to send a text message?
d) What was that all about? Why are you getting so angry?
e) Would you like me to pick you up?
f) Would you mind telling her I called?
g) You couldn't lend me £10, could you?
h) You've been working for twelve hours now.

B

1 Calm down. We've got plenty of time.
2 Er, sorry, I'm skint.
3 I've really had enough of him. Why can't he act his age?
4 Of course, no problem. Er, hold on. Who's speaking?
5 So what? It won't kill me.
6 That's all right, thanks. I'll get the bus.
7 To be honest, I don't know much about mobile phones.
8 Yeah, great. We're really enjoying ourselves.

Vocabulary

1 Look at the picture and say if the sentences are true (T) or false (F).

Example

A woman is walking down the street with her pet dog. ☐T☐

a) She has wrinkles and false eyelashes. ☐

b) Her hair is straight and dyed blond. ☐

c) She is wearing a fur coat. ☐

d) There are bodyguards on either side of her. ☐

e) Both bodyguards have got beards. ☐

f) One of the bodyguards looks like an old hippy. ☐

g) One of the bodyguards is fighting with some protesters. ☐

h) There are dozens of protesters on the street. ☐

i) The protesters are demonstrating about fur coats. ☐

j) One protester is pointing at the woman. ☐

k) The woman does not want to take a leaflet. ☐

l) The protesters have put posters on the wall. ☐

m) There is a lot of litter on the street. ☐

2 Complete each sentence with a word from the box. You can use the words more than once.

off   out   over   through   up

Example
We need to find <u>out</u> what time the train leaves.

a) At first, she was very sad, but she soon got _____ it.

b) Cheer _____ , Philip! Life isn't that bad!

c) He's not serious – he's just winding you _____ .

d) I tried to speak to him on the phone all day yesterday but I could never get _____ .

e) She gave _____ smoking on January 1st.

f) Students must switch _____ their mobile phones during the lessons.

g) The demonstration started peacefully but fighting broke _____ later.

h) The teacher handed _____ the question papers and the test began.

3 Put the missing words in the grid below to find the hidden word in the grey boxes.

Example
Can you show me how to ..... a message on my voicemail?

a) We had a great time, we really ..... ourselves.

b) Can you turn up the ..... ? I can't hear.

c) He will ..... a lot of money when his grandmother dies.

d) Tom Cruise ..... in *Mission Impossible*.

e) Her ..... is not serious but she needs to take a few days off work.

f) ..... vegetables are not treated with chemicals.

g) He had been a very ..... boy and his parents were angry with him.

	R	E	C	O	R	D
a)		N				D
b)		O			E	
c)		N				T
d)		T				D
e)		L				S
f)		R				C
g)		A				Y

4 Circle the best alternative.

Example
Does he never (get) / have / make tired of talking?

a) At first, I enjoyed it but then I *got / had / made* bored.
b) He lost his job and quickly *got / had / made* into debt.
c) I *got / had / made* a bit of difficulty with the test.
d) I *got / had / made* an interesting conversation with my boss yesterday.
e) I need to *get / have / make* a phone call to my bank.
f) She *got / had / made* an argument with her boyfriend.
g) The children *get / have / make* very frightened in the dark.
h) The crowd *got / had / made* a lot of noise when the team came onto the pitch.
i) Why do you always *get / have / make* such a mess?

5 Make nouns from the following words.

Example
  confident   _confidence_

a) cruel   _____
b) demonstrate   _____
c) difficult   _____
d) educate   _____
e) explain   _____
f) explosive   _____
g) inform   _____
h) legalise   _____
i) mysterious   _____
j) pollute   _____
k) scientific   _____
l) traditional   _____

6 Complete each sentence with a noun from exercise 5.

Example
A lot of _pollution_ in cities is caused by traffic.

a) A recent survey showed that most people have no _____ in the government.
b) He completed his _____ at Manchester University.
c) I'd like some _____ about language courses in Ireland.
d) It was a violent _____ and there were many arrests.
e) Many politicians now support the _____ of some drugs.

f) The students had no _____ with the exercise and finished quickly.
g) The teacher began the lesson with an _____ of the grammar rules.
h) They were protesting about _____ to animals.

7 Replace the words in *italics* with their opposites from the box and rewrite the story.

careless	cold	fast	front	narrow		
never	rude	unfortunately	violent	wet		

It was a *warm*, *dry* day and we were driving *slowly* down a *wide* street in the town. My husband is a *careful* driver and he *always* stops at red lights. Suddenly, another car drove into the *back* of our Mercedes. *Fortunately*, my husband is a very *peaceful* man, and he's always very *polite*. He got out of the car ….

It was a cold, wet day and we …

_____
_____
_____
_____
_____
_____
_____
_____
_____
_____
_____

8 Find and correct twelve spelling mistakes in the story below.

A man went to the dentist for his anual check-up and took a seat in the crowded waiting room. As useual, he was very woried and sat nerviously waiting his turn. Finaly, the receptionist told him to follow her into the surgery.

The dentist carefuly examined the man's teeth, turned to the patient and said, 'There's absolutely nothing rong with your teeth. But I would like to ask you to do me a favour.'

'Of course,' replyed the man.

'I'd like you to screem really loudly – really, really loudly.'

'Why?' asked the patient.

'Well, the waiting room is full of poeple who want to see me and I want to go to a consert this evening.'

_annual_____   _____   _____
_____   _____   _____
_____   _____   _____
_____   _____   _____

16 Lifestyle

Grammar

1 An advertisement for a health farm made the following promises. Insert *will* in an appropriate place in each promise.

> ### After just two weeks with us ...
>
>   <u>will</u>
> you / lose at least five kilos.
>
> a) you be relaxed and positive about life.
>
> b) you feel younger and healthier.
>
> c) your energy levels be much higher.
>
> d) relationships with your friends be happier.
>
> e) your general fitness improve.
>
> f) you change the way you think about food.
>
> g) your friends think you look wonderful.

2 A man has booked two weeks at the health farm.

Do you think the farm will keep its promises? Change four sentences in exercise 1 by
- inserting *probably* or *definitely* and/or
- making the sentences negative to show what you think will happen.

Example
He probably won't lose at least five kilos.

3 Put the verbs into the appropriate form (simple present or *will* + infinitive).

Example
As soon as he <u>leaves</u> (leave) the farm, he'll have a cigarette.

a) His wife will be happy when he _____ (come) home.

b) If she asks if he liked it, he _____ (say) yes.

c) When it _____ (be) six o'clock, he will go to the pub.

d) When his friends see him, they _____ (think) he is ill.

e) He really will be ill if he _____ (lose) any more weight.

f) When he _____ (eat) normally again, he'll put on weight.

g) If his wife _____ (ask) him to go to the health farm again, he'll say no.

4 Put the verbs into the appropriate form (simple present or *will* + infinitive).

Example
When we <u>get</u> (get) to Havana, a friend <u>will meet</u> (meet) us in the arrivals hall.

a) If he _____ (not be) there, we _____ (take) a taxi.

b) You _____ (have) to speak Spanish if the driver _____ (not speak) English!

c) When we _____ (get) to the hotel, I _____ (call) room service for a bottle of champagne.

d) As soon as we _____ (be) ready, we _____ (look) for a restaurant.

e) We _____ (go) to an expensive restaurant if you _____ (want).

f) If it _____ (not be) too late after the meal, we _____ (find) a place to listen to music.

g) I _____ (tell) you where I got the money when we _____ (get) back to London.

Reading

1 Read the article and match the paragraph headings to the paragraphs (A, B, C).

- Genetically modified fast food (*paragraph* ___)
- The danger to the environment (*paragraph* ___)
- What is added to your fast food? (*paragraph* ___)

2 Find the places (1–6) in the article where the following phrases should go.

a) do you know which chemicals you are eating? ☐

b) do you want to eat something that has been genetically modified? ☐

c) how much do you know about the fast food you eat? ☐1

d) in order to build farms ☐

e) maybe even the cow that the beef comes from ☐

f) Scientists can also make blue potatoes ☐

3 Complete the sentences with words from the article. The paragraph letter is given in brackets. The first letter of each word has been given to you.

Example
People on Okinawa e x p e c t to live to an old age.

a) What i _ _ _ _ _ _ _ _ _ _ do I need for this recipe? (A)

b) A diet with lots of fruit and vegetables is good for your h _ _ _ _ _ . (A)

c) R _ _ _ _ _ _ _ shows that there is a connection between smoking and many illnesses. (A)

d) If the p _ _ _ _ _ _ _ _ of fast food is not right, the food will go cold too quickly. (B)

e) The Green Party wants to protect the e _ _ _ _ _ _ _ _ _ _ _ . (B)

f) Nobody really knows if genetically m _ _ _ _ _ _ _ food is dangerous or not. (C)

TO EAT *or not to eat?*

At some time in the future, it is possible that people will look back to our time and remember it as the age of junk food. We all know that there are healthier ways to eat, but that doesn't stop us from spending billions of dollars on hamburgers and hot dogs. But ....(1)....

A You should expect to find a lot of chemical ingredients in fast food. None of them are good for your health, but not all of them are bad. Chlorine is used to make bread white. Cochineal (made from dried insects) is used to make things red. However, more research is needed to find out exactly how these chemicals will affect our health in years to come. The question is: ....(2)....

B Fast food and packaging come together. When you've eaten the burger, you throw away the packaging and somebody somewhere will then burn or bury it. This is clearly a problem for the environment. Fast food also contributes to global warming. In Brazil, 12 million acres of forest have been cut down ....(3).... . Farmers use this land to grow soya beans and the soya is given to the cows that become the beef in your beefburger. Fewer forests = more global warming. The question is: do you care?

C A lot of fast food contains ingredients that have been genetically modified. The tomatoes in the tomato sauce, the flour in the bread, ...(4).... – all of these can be changed by scientists to be very different. How is it possible that you can buy a bright red tomato in London, that comes from Cyprus, that is still fresh after four weeks? Dutch scientists have grown blue roses. ....(5).... Some of the ideas are strange but the changes are not always bad. Some plants can be modified to provide more vitamin C, for example. The question is: ....(6).... .

Vocabulary

1 Complete each question with a word or phrase from the box.

> ~~a diet~~   fit   a healthy life   holiday
> stress   a walk   weight   yoga
> your fitness

Example
Have you ever been on _a diet_?

a) Do you think that you lead _____?

b) Do you need to improve _____?

c) What do you do to keep _____?

d) When did you last go for _____?

e) Would you like to lose _____?

f) Have you ever done _____?

g) How well do you cope with _____?

h) What do you usually do on _____?

2 Answer each question with a word from the box.

> aubergine   carrot   chicken   cucumber
> garlic   grape   lettuce   ~~peach~~   pepper
> prawn   sausage   spinach   trout

Example
Which is a fruit that grows on trees? _peach_

a) Which is a green leaf that contains lots of iron? _____

b) Which is used to make wine? _____

c) Which is a river fish? _____

d) Which lives in the sea, but is not a fish? _____

e) Which is a vegetable that can be red or green? _____

f) Which looks like a small onion? _____

g) Which is orange and grows under ground? _____

h) Which is purple on the outside and white inside? _____

i) Which is dark green on the outside and pale green inside? _____

j) Which is a green leaf that is usually used in salads? _____

k) Which is a bird? _____

l) Which is made of chopped meat? _____

3 Complete the phrases by matching a verb on the left with a phrase on the right.

a) baked   1   in a blender
b) boiled   2   in batter
c) chopped   3   in a litre of water
d) eaten   4   very thinly
e) fried   5   in the oven
f) grilled   6   into small cubes
g) mixed   7   on a barbecue
h) sliced   8   raw

4 Complete each sentence with a word from the box.

> calorie   ~~frozen~~   junk   recipe   snack
> starving   vitamins

Example
It's very easy to cook _frozen_ food in the microwave oven.

a) He went on a low-_____ diet because he wanted to lose a few kilos.

b) Many teenagers love _____ food, like chips and chocolate.

c) Could you give me the _____ for that dish?

d) We often have a little _____ between lunch and dinner.

e) I'm absolutely _____ – what time is dinner?

f) You must eat lots of vegetables to get all the _____ you need.

5 Complete each sentence with an idiom from the box.

> ~~driving me nuts~~   full of beans
> not my cup of tea   packed in like sardines
> a piece of cake

Example
Stop doing that! It's _driving me nuts_ .

a) Cricket is very popular in England but it's _____

b) The buses are terrible in the morning – you're _____

c) We finished it in about two seconds – it was _____

d) You're really energetic today – why are you so _____

Writing

Look at the pictures and write the story of Toby's visit to a health farm. Use the questions to help you.

Begin your story like this:

Toby was unfit and overweight and, one day, his wife gave him a surprise birthday present: one week at a health farm! When ...

Picture 1
What was Toby doing when he arrived at the health farm?
What did the trainer say to him? Why?

Picture 2
How much did Toby weigh on the first morning?
What did his trainer tell him?

Picture 3
When did Toby go to the canteen?
What did he have for lunch?
How did he feel?

Picture 4
What did everybody do in the afternoon?
What happened to Toby?

Picture 5
Who did Toby telephone that evening? Why?
What did he order?
Where did he eat his dinner?
How did he feel?

Picture 6
How much did he weigh at the end of the week? Why?
How did his trainer feel? Why?

Pronunciation

Look at the underlined letters. Which letters in each group of words are pronounced differently? Circle them.

Example

(au)bergine c**au**liflower s**au**sage

a) b**ea**ns   br**ea**k   cr**ea**m
b) h**ea**lth   h**ea**ven   p**ea**ch
c) bel**ie**ve   fr**ie**nd   p**ie**ce
d) n**ei**ghbour   w**ei**ght   rec**ei**ve
e) abr**oa**d   appr**oa**ch   t**oa**st
f) c**ou**ch   tr**ou**t   y**ou**th
g) c**ou**ntry   m**ou**ntain   tr**ou**ble

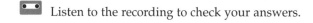 Listen to the recording to check your answers.

17 Animals

Grammar

1 The sentences below were written by English schoolchildren in their examinations. Complete each sentence with a relative pronoun (*who* or *that*). Only use *that* when *who* is not possible.

Example
A fjord is a car <u>that</u> is made in Scandinavia.

a) Charles Darwin was the naturalist _____ wrote 'The Organ of the Species'.

b) Electric volts are named after Voltaire, the man _____ invented electricity.

c) Euthanasia is the part of Asia _____ is nearest to Europe.

d) H_2O is water _____ is hot, and CO_2 is cold.

e) Handel was a composer _____ was half German, half Italian and half English.

f) Karl Marx was a comedian _____ made funny films with his brothers.

g) The boats _____ are seen in Venice are called gorgonzolas.

h) William Tell is the man _____ invented the telephone.

Can you see what is factually wrong in each sentence?

2 Circle the correct alternative: *that, it, they* or nothing (–).

Once upon a time, there was a baby camel (*that*)/ *it* lived in a zoo. One day, he turned to his father and said, 'Dad, what's the name of this big thing (a) *that* / *it* is on my back?'

'It's a hump, son,' replied the father. 'It's a kind of food store (b) *that* / *it* you need (c) *it* / – when you're in the desert.'

'Dad,' he said again, 'what do you call these hairs (d) *that* / *they* are above my eyes?'

'They're eyelashes, son. They protect your eyes from the wind that you get (e) *it* / – in the desert,' said his dad.

'Dad,' he asked, 'why have I got feet (f) *that* / *they* are bigger than all the other animals?'

'The sand (g) *that* / *it* you get (h) *it* / – in the desert is very soft,' said his dad. 'Your big feet help you to walk.'

'Oh, thanks, Dad,' said the baby camel. 'So, why do we live in a zoo?'

3 Complete each question with the correct form of the verb in brackets.

Example
If you <u>saw</u> (see) an injured bird in the street, would you help it?

a) If there was a mosquito in your bedroom, _____ (you try) to kill it?

b) If a cat _____ (come) into your house, would you give it something to eat?

c) If a friend _____ (invited) you to a bull fight, would you go?

d) If you found a spider in the bath, what _____ (you do)?

e) If a friend _____ (ask) you to look after their dog for two weeks, what would you say?

f) If the government closed all the zoos in your country, how _____ (you feel)?

g) If someone asked you to give some money to a hospital for sick animals, how much _____ (you give)?

Now answer the questions so that they are true for you.

Example
Yes, I would. I'd take it to a vet.

_____

_____

_____

_____

_____

_____

_____

_____

_____

Listening

1 📼 Cover the tapescript opposite and listen to a comedian telling jokes about a dog. Put the pictures in the correct order.

Have I ever told you about my dog? I never really wanted a dog, but I was in a department store one day last week and I had to go to the top floor where they sell books. I was looking for a good book of jokes. Anyway, I found the escalator, and there was a sign and it said 'Dogs must be carried'. 'What do I do?' I thought, 'I haven't got a dog.' Anyway, I found the pet department, which was on the ground floor and bought myself a dog. You don't want to break the rules, do you? And what a dog! The most intelligent dog I've ever seen. When we got to the book department, there was a sign on the wall. 'Wet paint' it said. The dog looked at the sign, barked 'woof woof', lifted his leg and, well, yes, he did. He actually did it right there on the wall. 'Wow,' I said, 'a dog that can read.' The dog looked at me and you know what? He spoke! 'I can speak, too,' he said. This was just too much. A talking dog! I couldn't believe it. I took him back to the pet department and I said to the man at the counter, I said, 'Did you know you have just sold me a dog that can read and talk?' 'Yes, I know,' said the man, 'but he's not very intelligent. When we play chess, I usually win.'

The next day, the next day, I took the dog to a job centre. 'Look,' I said to the woman in the job centre, 'I've got this dog that can read, do tricks, talk, he can type sixty words a minute and he wants a job.' The woman looked at me and looked at the dog. 'What languages do you speak?' she asked. 'Well,' said the dog, 'I can talk English and I can talk dog.' 'Anything else?' asks the woman. 'Yes, of course,' says the dog, 'Miaow.'

2 📼 Listen again and choose the best answer to the questions below.

Example
Why did the man go to the department store?
a) to buy a dog
b) to buy a book ✓

1 Why did he have to take the escalator?
   a) because he had a dog
   b) because he needed the top floor

2 How did he know that the dog could read?
   a) the dog wet the paint
   b) the dog told him he could read

3 Why didn't the man in the pet department think the dog was very intelligent?
   a) the dog usually lost when they played chess
   b) he knew how to play chess

4 Why did the man take the dog to the job centre?
   a) because he wanted a job
   b) because he wanted a job for the dog

Vocabulary

1 Search the word square (↑ ↓ → ←) for twenty-four names of animals.

E	O	T	I	U	Q	S	O	M	P	L	H
L	S	D	S	P	I	D	E	R	A	O	S
E	N	O	P	W	B	E	A	R	R	O	I
P	A	L	I	O	R	E	E	D	R	N	F
H	K	P	G	C	C	A	T	E	O	H	E
A	E	H	T	C	E	S	N	V	T	A	S
N	E	I	P	E	N	D	A	I	N	M	I
T	F	N	H	A	T	E	E	H	C	S	O
T	F	F	T	I	E	S	R	O	H	T	T
N	A	L	N	O	C	A	M	E	L	E	R
A	R	O	O	R	A	G	N	A	K	R	O
F	I	D	O	G	I	G	U	A	N	A	T
S	G	R	A	T	E	L	I	T	P	E	R

mosquito _____ _____

ant _____ _____

reptile _____ _____

_____ _____ _____

_____ _____ _____

_____ _____ _____

_____ _____ _____

2 Use the names of the animals in the word square to answer the questions.

Example
Which animal do we get malaria from?

m o s q u i t o

a) Which animal barks? _ _ _
b) Which animal spins a web? _ _ _ _ _ _
c) Which animal is long and sometimes venomous? _ _ _ _ _
d) Which animal carries its baby in a pocket?

 _ _ _ _ _ _ _
e) Which animal is a colourful bird?

 _ _ _ _ _ _
f) Which animal eats leaves from the top of trees? _ _ _ _ _ _ _
g) Which animal is the fastest runner?

 _ _ _ _ _ _ _
h) Which animal do we put a saddle on when we want to ride it? _ _ _ _ _

3 Circle the correct word.

Example
Do you know the fairy *tail* /(*tale*)about the princess and the frog?

a) We had to *wait* / *weight* two hours for the train.
b) Bambi was a baby *dear* / *deer*.
c) Why don't you *right* / *write* him a letter?
d) When we were in the mountains we saw a huge black *bare* / *bear*.
e) Gorillas have an average *wait* / *weight* of about 160 kilos.

4 Choose the best alternative to complete each sentence.

Example
I've always been very <u>interested</u> in reptiles.
fascinated   interested   keen

a) I get very _____ of all the animal documentaries on TV.
   bored   interested   worried

b) Are you _____ of snakes?
   afraid   disapprove   fascinated

c) He's really _____ on the idea of going on safari.
   interested   keen   thinking

d) Are you _____ about environmental problems?
   interested   tired   worried

e) I had a mynah bird but I got _____ of it talking all the time.
   disapprove   fascinated   tired

f) Do you _____ of keeping animals in zoos?
   approve   think   worry

g) We were _____ by the way the dog did tricks.
   fascinated   keen   tired

h) What do you _____ about getting a hamster as a pet?
   approve   think   interest

Writing

1 Look at the letter below and choose the best pet for Bill from the photos opposite.

I am a retired manager. I am 74 years old, but I am in very good health. I have been a little lonely since my wife died and I am sometimes frightened in the house on my own. I live in the country and enjoy going for walks. I don't like cats but I love all other animals. What pet do you recommend?

Bill Bowell

2 Now read the reply below. Does the writer agree with you? Does the writer have the same reasons as you?

I am convinced that that the best pet for Bill is a dog.

In the first place, dogs make very good companions and Bill will be less lonely.

Secondly, Bill enjoys going for walks, so he could take the dog with him. *Finally,* dogs are helpful to protect people in their homes.

It seems to me that hamsters and goldfish are *completely unsuitable.* They do not communicate and I do not think they will improve Bill's life. A cat is *clearly out of the question because* Bill doesn't like them.

In my opinion, therefore, a dog is *the best choice.* A dog will solve Bill's problems and make him a happier man.

3 Read the letter below and choose the best pet for Zoë.

I am twelve years old and I share a room with my twin brother, Arthur. Arthur has got a pet mouse and I want a pet, too. I want something cute and cuddly. We live in a twelfth floor flat in central Manchester. My parents have agreed to get me a pet, but they have told me that I must look after it. They don't like animals and it must stay in my room.

Zoë Houseman

Write a short reply and explain which pet you think is best for Zoë. Give your reasons.
Use the reply in exercise 2 to help you and use as many of the expressions in *italics* as possible.

Pronunciation

The words in *italics* in each pair of sentences have different pronunciations and different meanings. Decide how to pronounce these words.

1 a) Do you live *close* to the school?
   b) What time does the school *close*?

2 a) They *live* near the TV studios.
   b) There's a *live* concert of U2 on TV tonight.

3 a) Can you show me how to *use* this phone?
   b) It's not much *use* – it doesn't work!

4 a) They prefer to sit in the back *row* of the cinema.
   b) They had a big *row* last night.

5 a) I really *object* to his behaviour.
   b) An intransitive verb does not have an *object*.

6 a) I'm going to visit my *Polish* friend in Warsaw next week.
   b) He likes to *polish* his car every weekend.

▢▢ Listen to the recording to check your answers.

18 *Weird*

Grammar

1 Read the sentences. In each case, tick (✓) which happened first, a) or b).

Example
It was late when I got home because I had worked late at the office.
a) I got home   b) I worked late at the office ✓

1 *I had had a quick meal and I switched on the TV for the late night movie, 'Alien Killers'.*
   a) I had a meal   b) I switched on the TV

2 *I went to bed as soon as the film had finished.*
   a) I went to bed   b) The film finished

3 *I saw a bright light at my window after I had got into bed.*
   a) I saw a bright light   b) I got into bed

4 *I had closed the windows but there was a strong wind in my room.*
   a) I closed the windows
   b) There was a strong wind

5 *When the wind had gone away, I heard a strange voice.*
   a) The wind went away
   b) I heard a strange voice

6 *When the voice had spoken, the bright light disappeared.*
   a) The voice spoke
   b) The bright light disappeared

2 Make sentences in the past perfect using the verbs in brackets.

Example
I felt very ill.
I <u>had eaten</u> (eat) too much.

a) He looked very white.
    He _____ (see) a ghost.

b) She was late for work.
    She _____ (miss) the bus.

c) She woke up suddenly.
    She _____ (have) a bad dream.

d) I did very badly in the exam.
    I _____ (not study) very much.

e) They finally got married.
    They _____ (be engaged) for five years.

3 Circle the correct verb form.

On 28 July 1900, King Umberto I of Italy (visited) / had visited a restaurant in Monza. He (a) *arrived / had arrived* in the town earlier that day. He had his dinner and then (b) *spoke / had spoken* to the restaurant owner, also called Umberto. He (c) *discovered / had discovered* that they (d) *were / had been* born in the same town on the same day. The king introduced his wife, whose name (e) *was / had been* Margherita. The name of the restaurant owner's wife (f) *was / had been* Margherita, too. They then (g) *discovered / had discovered* another amazing coincidence. Both couples (h) *got married / had got married* on the same day, more than 30 years previously.

The day after their meeting, the king was very sad to learn that the restaurant owner (i) *died / had died* in a shooting accident. He was turning to his assistant to ask about the funeral, when he (j) *heard / had heard* a shot from a gun. King Umberto died instantly – the victim of an assassination.

4 Put the verbs in brackets into the correct form (simple past or past perfect).

In 1887, Lucy Dodson <u>was</u> (be) in bed when she (a) _____ (hear) a voice call her name. She (b) _____ (realise) that it was the voice of her mother who (c) _____ (die) 16 years previously. She (d) _____ (look) up and saw that her mother was carrying two small children in her arms. The ghost (e) _____ (ask) Lucy to look after the children because they (f) _____ (lose) their mother. Lucy (g) _____ (take) the children into her bed, but when she woke up in the morning, the bed was empty and the children (h) _____ (go). Two days later, Lucy learnt that her sister-in-law (i) _____ (die) that same night, leaving two small children. She later (j) _____ (discover) that her mother's ghost had appeared to her just two hours after her sister-in-law's death.

Reading

1 Match the paragraph beginnings 1–6 with the paragraph endings a–f opposite to tell the story. The paragraph beginnings are in the correct order.

1 One morning in March 1889, a man called Ansel Bourne woke up feeling confused. ...

2 'Good morning, Mr Brown,' said the people in the newspaper shop. ...

3 'Go and get Mr Brown a chair,' said a man in the shop. ...

4 When the reply arrived, everybody was shocked. ...

5 Two months earlier, on 17 January, Mr Ansel Bourne had left his home early in the morning. ...

6 For two months, Bourne's family in Greene had tried to find him. ...

2 Read the story again and put the events below in the order in which they happened.

a) He arrived in a town 200 miles from his home.
b) He asked the people to telephone his family.
c) He disappeared.
d) He returned to his old life.
e) He went to a bank and took out some money.
f) He went to work in a newspaper shop.
g) He woke up one morning and felt very confused.
h) People that he didn't recognise said 'Good morning' to him.

1	2	3	4	5	6	7	8
e							d

Mr Bourne or Mr Brown?

a ... 'He's not feeling well.' Mr Bourne told them his name again and asked them to contact his family in Greene. The staff in the shop wanted to keep him happy so they sent a telegram to Greene.

b ... By March everybody thought that thieves had killed him and stolen the money that he had taken out of the bank. Bourne returned home to his old life. He had no memory of the day he had disappeared and he was never able to explain why he had gone to Pennsylvania.

c ... He had gone to the bank, taken some money out of his account and immediately disappeared. A few days later Mr A.J. Brown arrived in Norristown and bought a newspaper shop on the main street. It was the same man.

d ... He was in a strange bed in a strange apartment. How had he got there? He had no idea. He knew his name and that he lived in Greene, Rhode Island, but that was all he knew. He got up, got dressed, had some breakfast and walked down the street to a newspaper shop. He wasn't really sure why, but he felt that he had to go there. He found that he was in the town of Norristown, Pennsylvania, 200 miles from Greene.

e ... They seemed to know him, but he had never seen them before. He told them that his name was Bourne. They thought he was joking, but it was soon clear that he was being serious.

f ... The man really was Ansel Bourne and his family had almost given up hope of finding him again. But for two months, the people of Norristown had known him as Mr Brown, the owner of the newspaper shop on their main street.

Vocabulary

1 Complete each question with a word from the box.

> far ~~fast~~ long many much often
> old well

Example

How _fast_ can you drive on motorways in your country?

a) How _____ people are there in your class?

b) How _____ is the youngest student in your class?

c) How _____ do you know your teacher?

d) How _____ does your teacher give you homework?

e) How _____ does it take you to get to school?

f) How _____ is your home from your school?

g) How _____ did you pay for this book?

Now answer the questions.

2 Complete the sentences with *have*, *make* or *take*.

Example

People say that teachers and doctors _have_ lots in common.

a) A professional photographer came to _____ photos of the wedding.

b) He's going to _____ a course in Business English.

c) Her secretary will _____ all the travel arrangements.

d) I _____ no idea what causes crop circles.

e) I'd love to _____ a go at flying a helicopter.

f) Ladies and gentlemen, please _____ your seats.

g) They hope to _____ a lot of money with their new company.

h) This government does not _____ promises that it cannot keep.

3 Complete each sentence with a word or phrase from the box.

> embarrassed   excited   ~~exhausted~~
> frightened   in a bad mood   jealous
> on top of the world   proud   sad

Example

He had run more than ten kilometres and he was feeling _exhausted_.

a) He was _____ because she went to see her old boyfriend.

b) I was so _____ when I forgot his name.

c) I'm _____ because I had a lot of problems at work today.

d) It was the first time he had done a marathon and felt very _____ of himself.

e) Many people were very _____ when they heard that the princess had died.

f) She had a lovely family, wonderful friends and a fantastic job and she was feeling _____ .

g) There was only one more day before the party and the children were feeling very _____ .

h) We were lost in a dark forest and we began to feel very _____ .

4 Complete the story by changing the verbs in brackets to nouns.

Government officials are investigating the _disappearance_ (disappear) of a top secret spy plane during a training (a) _____ (fly) last week. Colonel Vance Arkin of the US Air Force, who is leading the (b) _____ (investigate), says there are a number of possible (c) _____ (explain). One theory is that the plane did not have (d) _____ (permit) to fly over a nuclear testing site in Nevada, controlled by the US Army, and that it was shot down. However, the army says that it has no record in its radar log of a plane that matches the (e) _____ (describe) of the spy plane. The Air Force has spent billions of dollars on the (f) _____ (develop) of this plane and officials are worried that this accident will damage public (g) _____ (confide) in the project.

Writing

Complete the story. Answer the questions and use your imagination.

THE WEATHER WAS BAD ON THE DAY OF THE FUNERAL. THERE WAS ONLY ONE PERSON THERE AND HE HAD PUT A SINGLE ROSE ON THE COFFIN...

Who had died? When? How had he/she died?
Who was the man at the funeral? Why was he there?
Why had nobody else come to the funeral?

NOBODY IS TOO SURE ABOUT EXACTLY WHAT HAPPENED. WHEN THE POLICE ARRIVED, THEY SAW...

What did the police see when they arrived?
Where was the spaceship shining its light?
What had happened to the man with the dark glasses?

THREE THOUSAND LIGHT YEARS AWAY AN ALIEN HAD JUST ARRIVED AT A PARTY.

Where was the party?
Why was everybody happy at the party?
What happened next?

Pronunciation

🔊 Read and listen to the mini-dialogue below.

– *We've got Ben Crystal with us here in the studio.*
– *Sorry, my name is **Ken** Crystal.*

The word *Ken* is stressed because it is the most important word in the sentence.

Look at the following mini-dialogues and decide which word (or words) is stressed in the second lines.

a) – Ken, you say you've visited many crop circles.
   – Yes, I've seen about a thousand.

b) – When were the first crop circles reported?
   – The first crop circle was seen in 1980.

c) – What time yesterday afternoon did you find the circle?
   – Actually, we found it in the morning.

d) – Do you think this crop circle was caused by the weather?
   – No, we think it was made by aliens.

e) – This circle is very big, isn't it?
   – Yes, it's more than a kilometre wide!

f) – Is this crop circle like all the others?
   – No, I've never seen one like this.

🔊 Listen to the recording to check your answers.

19 Wheels

Grammar

1 In the sentences below, replace the past simple with *used to* + infinitive **where it is possible**.

Example
As a child, I cycled to school every day.
As a child, I used to cycle to school every day.

a) The roads were quiet and safe.
_____

b) My parents gave me a racing bike for my tenth birthday.
_____

c) I was very proud of my bike.
_____

d) I cleaned it every day.
_____

e) My best friend was a boy called Tom.
_____

f) One day, I lent my him bike.
_____

g) He gave it back to me a week later.
_____

h) One wheel was broken and it was all dirty.
_____

2 Rearrange the words to make suggestions and advice for a person who is going to study English in London.

Example
a club don't join sports there Why you
Why don't you join a sports club there?

a) a choose good I I'd If language school were you
_____
_____

b) a could for job look there You
_____
_____

c) an don't English family stay Why with you
_____
_____

d) go I I'd If in the were winter you
_____
_____

3 Write five sentences with *used to / didn't use to* + infinitive comparing city life now and city life at the beginning of the 20th century. You can use the pictures to help you.

Examples
There used to be horses on the road.
People didn't use to drive to work.

_____
_____
_____
_____
_____
_____

Listening

1 📼 Cover the tapescript opposite and listen to three people talking about their dream cars. Match the speaker to the cars.

2 📼 Which of the topics below do the speakers discuss? Listen again and put a tick (✓) or a cross (✗) next to the topics for each speaker.

	Speaker 1	Speaker 2	Speaker 3
What colour is it?	✗		
What special features has it got?	✓		
How fast does it go?			
Where would you like to go in your car?			
Who would you take with you?			

3 📼 Either listen again or look at the tapescript and write short note-form answers to the questions in the table in exercise 2.

Vocabulary

1 Complete each sentence with a word from the box.

> belts bonnet boot ~~bumper~~ engine
> gear seats steering wheel
> windscreen wipers

Example
Cars have a <u>bumper</u> at the front and the back for protection in an accident.

a) A driver has to take one hand off the _____ wheel to change _____ .

b) All cars have safety _____ for the front _____ , and new cars have them in the back, too.

c) In most cars the _____ is under the _____ at the front of the car.

d) Many cars have a spare _____ in the _____ .

e) When it's raining, you need to switch on the _____ _____ .

2 Combine a word from box A with a word from box B to make compound nouns. Then complete the sentences with these compound nouns.

A

> air
> ~~city~~
> driving
> fast
> hair
> health
> public
> summer
> traffic

B

> care
> food
> conditioning
> ~~centre~~
> holiday
> jam
> licence
> style
> transport

Example
It's very difficult to park in the <u>city centre</u>.

a) _____ in the city is excellent, with good buses and a fast metro system.

b) All the rooms in the hotel have _____ .

c) I almost didn't recognise her with her new _____ .

d) I'm sorry I'm late – there was a huge _____ in the town centre.

e) Many traditional restaurants have closed because more and more people are eating _____ .

f) The government is planning to spend more on _____ and open three new hospitals.

g) The school is closed during the _____ .

h) You have to take a test before you get a _____ .

3 Complete each sentence with an adverb from the box.

> abroad casually closely dangerously
> heavily intelligently ~~occasionally~~
> partly specially

Example
He <u>occasionally</u> cooks a meal for his friends.

a) He was driving _____ and the police stopped him.

b) I admit I was _____ to blame for the accident.

c) It was raining _____ this morning.

d) People dress very _____ in the office where she works – jeans and trainers.

e) She _____ resembles her mother – people often think they are sisters.

f) The article was _____ written, but it was hard to understand.

g) The car was _____ designed for driving in cities.

h) We usually go _____ for our holidays.

4 Make adjectives from the nouns in brackets.

The new model is <u>economical</u> (economy) to run, but has a (a) _____ (power) 2.4 litre engine. It has a (b) _____ (space) interior and an (c) _____ (electricity) sun-roof for summer driving.

* * * *

Our city centres are (d) _____ (pollution) and crowded. But now there is another problem, with more and more (e) _____ (aggression) drivers on the roads. Many drivers seem to be less (f) _____ (consideration) than they used to be, and some people get (g) _____ (anger) for no reason at all. To be (h) _____ (safety), it is probably (i) _____ (wisdom) to lock your doors and keep the windows closed.

Writing

1 Read the letter opposite. What is the purpose of the letter?

- to give advice about hiring a car
- to give advice about travelling in England
- to give some personal news

2 Draw the itinerary that Pippa suggests on the map.

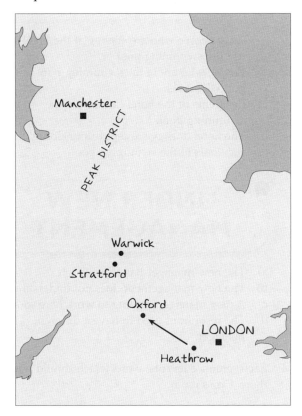

3 Underline in the letter opposite all the ways that Pippa gives advice and makes suggestions. An example has been done for you.

4 Look at this extract from a letter.

> It was very nice of you to invite me to come and stay with you. I've got a really cheap flight. It arrives a week before your holidays start, so I thought that I would spend a week travelling around the country. I'll come and see you after that. Have you got any good ideas? Where should I go?

Use Pippa's letter opposite as a model and reply to the letter above.

Dear Magda,

Many thanks for your letter. It was good to hear from you and it is fantastic news that you are coming to England. I think that it's a really good idea to spend a week travelling around the country before coming to see me.

If I were you, I'd hire a car. The trains are expensive and not very good, and the buses are slow. I suggest that you start in Oxford. It's a beautiful city and it's near the airport. And you could visit Eleanor while you're there. The next day, you could drive to Stratford and visit Shakespeare's birthplace and, if you have time afterwards, you could also visit Warwick Castle.

I know you like the countryside, so why don't you go to the Peak District after that? It's wonderful for walking and there aren't too many tourists. After that, Manchester is not far. It's got great night life – you'll love Canal Street! You probably won't have time for anything else, but when you're with me in London, we can visit a few more places.

Anyway, that's all for now. I hope I've given you a few ideas. I'll write again very soon.

All my love,
Pippa

Pronunciation

1 📼 Listen to two people speaking.

Which speaker sounds more positive? Which speaker uses a higher tone of voice?

2 📼 Listen to the recording and practise saying the sentences in a positive way.

a) I think my lessons are great fun.
b) The school I go to is excellent.
c) My English has really improved this year.
d) My teacher is the best in the world.

20 *Review 4*

Grammar

1 Look at the sign in each question and choose the best explanation.

① Closed for lunch
Back at 3.00

a) You can come back for lunch at 3 o'clock.
b) They will have lunch at 3 o'clock.
c) The shop will close after 3 o'clock.
d) The shop will open at 3 o'clock.

② WE NO LONGER ACCEPT CREDIT CARDS
Sorry for any inconvenience

a) They are going to accept credit cards soon.
b) They will only accept credit cards.
c) They used to accept credit cards.
d) They are sorry that the credit cards are very long.

③ *Smart dress*
NO TRAINERS OR T-SHIRTS

a) People who are wearing smart dresses cannot come in.
b) People who are wearing trainers or T-shirts cannot come in.
c) You must wear trainers or a T-shirt with your dress.
d) You can wear anything you want.

④ Insert key and immediately push door

a) Do not insert the key when you push the door.
b) Push the door as soon as you insert the key.
c) Insert the key when you push the door.
d) Push the key into the door immediately.

⑤ SEAVIEW HOTEL
THIS SWIMMING POOL IS FOR THE USE OF RESIDENTS ONLY

a) Only people who are staying at the hotel can use the swimming pool.
b) People who are in the swimming pool must go to the hotel.
c) Residents of the hotel cannot use the swimming pool.
d) The hotel does not accept responsibility for accidents in the swimming pool.

⑤ UNDER NEW MANAGEMENT

a) The new manager has recently left.
b) The new management does not understand.
c) A new manager is going to work here soon.
d) The restaurant used to have a different manager.

2 Each sentence has one word which should not be there. Cross it out.

Example
Could you explain ~~me~~ how to send an email?

a) We will have a break when we will finish this exercise.
b) That's the man I told you about him.
c) I've got a friend who she got married last week.
d) They were used to live in Madrid.
e) If you read more books, your English it would improve.
f) I would to see a doctor if I were you.
g) I hope I will to find a good job soon.
h) When he had finished breakfast, he had left for work.
i) She used to have wearing long, blond hair.
j) Why don't you speak to someone who he understands the problem?

3 Rewrite the sentences beginning with the words given.

Example
We're not allowed to smoke in the office
We must *not smoke in the office.*

a) Alex said, 'If I were you, I'd revise Unit 17.'
Alex said, 'Why don't _____

_____

b) The first student to finish will receive a prize.
The student who _____

_____

c) I'll finish my work and then I'll help you.
When I _____

_____

d) She peeled the potato and then sliced it.
When she had _____

_____

e) I'll give you a call when our train arrives.
As soon as _____

_____

f) My friend has invited me to visit – he lives in L.A.
My friend who _____

_____

g) A few years ago, this was a green field.
A few years ago this used _____

_____

4 Find a response in box B for the sentences in box A.

A

a) Are you in love with him?
b) But when will I find the time?
c) Should I tell him what I think?
d) Do you think you'll pass your exams?
e) Don't you think this is a bit boring?
f) Is there anything good on TV tonight?
g) What do you think of the new teacher?
h) When will you pay me back?
i) Why didn't you get a taxi?

B

1 Actually, I'm not very keen on her.
2 As soon as I get to the bank.
3 I didn't have enough cash on me.
4 I hope so.
5 I wouldn't if I were you.
6 No, but I used to be.
7 No, nothing special.
8 Well, you could take a day off work.
9 Yes, I'm sick of it.

5 Fill each gap with one word only.

You _have_ probably never heard of John Montagu, but he has another name (a) _____ is famous around the world. John Montagu, Earl of Sandwich, used (b) _____ spend a lot of his time playing cards. In fact, one day (c) _____ 1762, he played for more (d) _____ 24 hours without stopping. He wanted something that (e) _____ could eat while he (f) _____ playing. He (g) _____ given some meat and cheese between two slices (h) _____ bread. This meal became known (i) _____ the 'sandwich'. However, the sandwich is not the only thing (j) _____ carries his name. The Hawaiian Islands in the Pacific (k) _____ to be called the Sandwich Islands, and were named (l) _____ the famous card player. It is perhaps surprising (m) _____ he was honoured in this way. (n) _____ the time, Sandwich was the British Foreign Minister and many people thought that he (o) _____ responsible for losing the American War of Independence.

Vocabulary

1 Choose the best alternative from the options below to fill the gaps.

Casanova will always be <u>famous</u> for his success with the (a) _____ sex but few people really know much about this extraordinary (b) _____. He was born in 1725 and when he was sixteen he began a (c) _____ in the church. However, the church (d) _____ of his wild (e) _____ and he left Venice and the church.

In 1749, his (f) _____ with Henriette began. It was one of the most important in his life and it (g) _____ six months before they (h) _____. At this time, he developed a strong (i) _____ of friends who helped him return to Venice. He was soon in (j) _____ again and, for a (k) _____ , he was in prison. He managed to (l) _____ to France where he worked as a secret agent and was one of the founders of the first national lottery.

A life that was full of excitement and embarrassing (m) _____ followed. He travelled throughout Europe and (n) _____ ended up in Dux, in the Czech Republic, where he died in 1798.

Example

(famous)   good-looking   gorgeous

a) different   equal   opposite
b) ancestor   character   hamster
c) career   employer   profession
d) afraid   disapproved   worried
e) diet   lifestyle   meditation
f) girlfriend   partner   relationship
g) consisted   had   lasted
h) bored   exhausted   separated
i) network   timetable   web
j) problem   surprise   trouble
k) pause   run   while
l) arrange   escape   risk
m) incidents   intelligence   interiors
n) awfully   eventually   heavily

2 Complete the story with words from the box.

about   as   at   for   in   of   to   with

Janet Peto was fed up <u>with</u> her job as a waitress at a pizzeria in west London. She was sick (a) _____ doing the same thing every day and she wanted to have a go (b) _____ something new. She had thought (c) _____ doing a course in restaurant management, but she couldn't give (d) _____ her job because she needed the money.

One day, her favourite customer walked in. He was old enough to be her grandfather, but they had lots (e) _____ common and they often chatted. That evening, the old man ate his pizza (f) _____ usual, but he didn't seem interested (g) _____ talking. (h) _____ fact, he seemed to be very worried (i) _____ something. When he left, Janet went to clear his table. (j) _____ her surprise, she found a piece of paper under his plate. She picked it up and read: 'Dear Janet, I hope you will not object (k) _____ this present. You remind me (l) _____ my darling wife and I have always been very fond (m) _____ you. All my love, Alan Lawson.' She turned over the paper and saw that it was a cheque for £100,000.

Janet was unable (n) _____ thank him (o) _____ his present. She tried to call him on the phone, but there was no reply. He had died (p) _____ a heart attack (q) _____ his way home from the restaurant.

3 Complete each sentence by making an adjective from the word in brackets.

Example
He's a <u>dangerous</u> (danger) driver.

a) Male animals are often more _____ (aggression) than females.
b) They were not _____ (amusement) when they lost $100,000.
c) Why do you get _____ (anger) every time I make a mistake?
d) How _____ (belief) do you find the stories about crop circles?
e) She's got a _____ (jealousy) husband and she can't go out.
f) The car had leather seats and a _____ (space) interior.
g) His exam results were extremely _____ (surprise).

4 Replace the words in *italics* with their opposites from the box and rewrite the story.

> awful failure forgot full little
> nervous previous shy silly ~~unlucky~~
> weak

Maggie was always *lucky* with men and one day she tried a computer dating agency. She was looking for a *strong* personality because she was quite *out-going* herself. A week later, the agency found a man. They said he had *lots* in common with her and they were sure their first date would be a *success*.

Before going out, Maggie *remembered* to brush her teeth and put on her new perfume. She smelled *great*! Feeling quite *confident*, she arrived at the restaurant, which was almost *empty*. Then, she saw him, sitting at a table with a *serious* expression on his face. It was definitely him. It was her *future* husband!

Maggie was always unlucky with men …

---

5 Complete the crossword. You have seen all the words that you need in Units 16–19 of *Inside Out*. Some of the letters have been given to you.

Clues

Across
1 see picture 1 (10, 5)
6 see picture 6 (3)
8 see picture 8 (5)
9 past tense of *eat* (3)
10 animal that you keep in your house (3)
11 in a foreign country (6)
14 people from other planets (6)
15 place to record music or make films (6)
16 makes something happen (6)
18 see picture 18 (6)
19 instructions to make a meal (6)
21 animal hair (3)
22 see picture 22 (3)
23 not expensive (5)
24 put two numbers together (3)
25 system for keeping a building cold (3, 12)

Down
2 I have no idea! (1, 5'1, 1, 4)
3 see picture 3 (5)
4 people who know a lot about a subject (7)
5 not alive (4)
7 people who work with the law (7)
12 (and 19 down) anger between car drivers (4, 4)
13 quickly and without warning (3, 2, 1, 6)
15 weird (7)
17 food made with cooked vegetables or meat and water that you eat with a spoon (4)
18 cut into small pieces (past tense) (7)
19 see 12 down
20 see picture 20 (5)

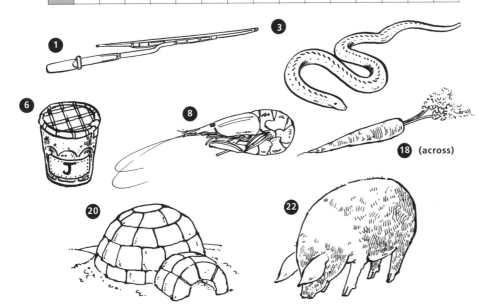

Answer key

1 Me

Grammar

1
1 What   Coppola
2 Which   Ringo Starr
3 Where   London
4 When   1977

2
a) Did you argue
b) Is that
c) Do you like
d) is your favourite Beatles song?
e) Do you think

3
a) How much *do you* weigh?
b) (no change)
c) How often *does* your teacher give you homework?
d) What *did* you have for breakfast today?
e) (no change)
f) (no change)

4
a) Why did David Bowie's son change his name?
b) Who named his daughter after a part of London?
c) How many languages does A.L.I.C.E. speak?
d) When did John Lennon record *Stand By Me*?

Answers
a) Because it was embarrassing.
b) Ex-US-President Bill Clinton.
c) Only English.
d) 1975.

Reading

1
a) The world's most inappropriate name
b) Will you marry me?
c) How stupid can you be?

2 a) 4 b) 1 c) 2 d) 3 e) 6 f) 5

3 *Suggested answers*
a) How many legs did the dog have?
b) What did the dog have around its neck?
c) What was Sir Thomas Beecham's job? / What did Sir Thomas Beecham do?
d) Which name couldn't Sir Thomas Beecham change?
e) When did they get married?
f) Where did Mrs Smith see the names?
g) When did she discover her terrible mistake?

Vocabulary

1 a) Mary b) Mimi c) Yoko d) Julia e) Yuka

2 a) True b) True c) False d) False e) False
f) False g) True h) False

3
a) correct b) correct
c) They looked ~~like~~ a bit tired after the lesson.
d) correct
e) She sounds ~~like~~ foreign – is she Greek?
f) correct
g) You look ~~like~~ stressed out. What's up?

4 a) 4 b) 7 c) 1 d) 3 e) 8 f) 2 g) 6 h) 5

5 a) used-car salesman b) doctor
c) police officer d) banker e) waiter
f) psychologist g) student h) au pair

Writing

1 Message a) languages, communicating, people
Message b) favourite (*or* favorite (US)), team, address
Message c) country, beautiful, beach
Message d) especially, writing, homework
Message e) improve, different, receiving

Pronunciation

1 mean – niece – feel   movie – improve – grew
sport – call – daughter   surname – learn – girl

2 a) part b) wheel / we'll c) tool d) first
e) born

2 Place

Grammar

1 *Plurals ending in 's'*
statues taxis tourists

Plurals ending in 'es'
brushes churches watches

Plurals ending in 'ies'
qualities summaries universities

Irregular plurals
men teeth women

2 a) progress b) luggage c) homework
d) information e) money f) bread g) air

3 a) much b) much c) much d) many
e) much f) many g) many
Students' own answers

4 a) much b) a little – True (usually)
c) many – False (most waiters and waitresses come from other countries)
d) a few – True e) a few – True
f) many – False (there is only one castle in London: the Tower of London)
g) much – False (London, especially Docklands in the east of London, is full of modern buildings)
h) much – False

Listening

1 Picture b

2 a) False – He first went to Marrakech ten to twelve years ago.
b) False – He went there for a (long) weekend.
c) False – He travelled with his best friend, Dave.
d) True
e) False – After dinner, he went to the market square.
f) False – Djemaa el Fna is the name of the market square.
g) True
h) True
i) False – He has been there ten or twelve times.
j) False – His last visit was three years ago.

Vocabulary

1 a) statue b) beach c) square d) office block
e) castle f) hill g) church h) fountain

2
things you like	things you don't like
amazing	ugly
spectacular	awful
lovely	disgusting
attractive	dull
exciting	miserable
fabulous	terrible
fantastic	useless
great	

3 a) French b) Japanese c) Hungarian d) Irish
e) Italian f) Portuguese g) Egyptian
h) Argentinian

4 a) in b) in c) on d) in e) on f) at g) on

Pronunciation

Oo	oO
happen	describe
label	discuss
listen	explain
mention	relax
practise	repeat
visit	suppose

Writing

1 Dear <u>Mum and Dad</u>,
I got here <u>a few days ago</u> and I'm having a <u>fabulous</u> time. The weather is <u>terrible</u>, but there are a few <u>lots</u> of things to do. There are a few <u>places of interest</u> near the hotel where I <u>go in the afternoon</u> and <u>take photographs</u>. I've met a <u>professor of archaeology</u> from <u>Helsinki</u> who is taking me to <u>some interesting ruins</u> tomorrow. The <u>food</u> is interesting – so different from at home. I'm always really tired in the <u>evening</u> after so much <u>sightseeing</u> – I'll need a holiday after this!
<u>Love</u>,
Simon

3 Couples

Grammar

1 a) met b) fell c) forgot d) were e) wanted
f) killed g) thought h) was i) woke
j) found k) took l) killed

2 a) Where did Romeo meet Juliet? / Where did Romeo and Juliet meet?
b) Who did Romeo forget about?
c) Who did Juliet's family want her to marry?
d) Who did Romeo kill?
e) Why did Romeo kill himself?
f) What did Juliet do when she woke up? / What happened when she woke up?
g) How did Juliet kill herself?

3 a) was holding b) was feeling c) was sitting
d) was hoping e) were speaking
f) was making g) was getting

4 a) was watching b) said
c) opened d) was sitting
e) began f) wanted g) was raining
h) decided i) arrived

Reading

1 1 B 2 D 3 C 4 A

2
1	2	3	4	5	6	7	8	9	10	11	12
d	h	c	l	a	g	i	k	j	e	b	f

3 *Suggested answers*
a) She met Onassis.
b) Because he treated her like a woman.
c) Because he was seeing other women.
d) She was reading the newspaper. / She saw it / read about it in the newspaper.
e) Because his marriage was not happy.
f) She was visiting Onassis's grave.

Vocabulary

1
1	2	3	4	5	6	7	8	9
a	c	e	i	b	g	d	h	f

2 a) dream b) marriage c) unfaithful d) lover
e) rumours f) affair g) divorced

3 a) have b) have c) have d) have e) get
f) get g) get

4 a) out b) up c) out d) out e) up f) up
g) out

Pronunciation

1 a) begun b) drank c) ran d) rung e) sung
f) sank g) swum

2 a) /riːd/ b) /red/ c) /red/

4 Fit

Grammar

1 a) happier b) hotter c) more successful
  d) better e) more interesting f) bigger
  g) worse

2 Rosa Jake Lizzie Daniel David

3 a) The biggest b) The luckiest c) the highest
  d) the most expensive e) the wettest
  f) the richest g) the most popular

4 Probably the *most* common health problem for men
  is heart disease. Exercise is important but not *as*
  important as a healthy diet. A bad diet is *the* biggest
  cause of this disease. Vegetables are better for you *than*
  fatty foods, but some vegetables are *more* useful than
  others. Supermarket products are *not* as healthy as
  organic produce. People with *the* most stressful jobs
  have shorter lives *than* people who are stress-free, so
  look for ways to relax. You should exercise more *than*
  once a week. A hard, sweaty sport is not *as* good
  for you *as* regular, gentle exercise.

Listening and reading

1 Picture a) Story 2
  Picture b) Story 3
  Picture c) Story 1

2 a) EE b) SK c) EE d) EM e) SK
  f) EM g) SK h) EE i) EM j) SK, EE

3 1 a) 2 a) 3 b) 4 a) 5 b) 6 b)

Vocabulary

1 a) boxing b) cyclist c) gymnast
  d) ice hockey player e) rower f) skiing
  g) squash

2 a) goes b) does c) does d) plays e) does
  f) goes g) goes h) plays i) goes

3 a) fortunate b) calm c) attractive d) fit
  e) average f) fun g) famous

4 a) Professional b) sweaty c) aerobic
  d) dangerous e) talented f) successful
  g) valuable

5 a) 6 b) 3 c) 7 d) 1 e) 4 f) 5 g) 2

Writing

1 A man was feeling unwell and he went to see the
  doctor. He went with his wife because he was a
  little worried. Afterwards the doctor spoke to the
  man's wife. He said, 'I'm afraid I have some bad
  news. Unless you follow my instructions very
  carefully, your husband will die. Every morning
  you must give him a good breakfast and you
  must cook him a healthy meal at night. What is
  more, you must not ask him to do any

housework and you must keep the house very
clean. It is a lot of work for you, but it really is the
only way to keep him alive.'

On the way home, the husband asked his
wife what the doctor had said to her. 'He said
you're going to die,' she replied.

2 One day a *bus* driver was in his *bus* when the
  biggest man he had ever seen got on. The giant
  looked at the driver, said, 'Big John *doesn't* pay,'
  and took his *seat* on the *bus*. The *bus* driver was
  only a *little* man and he did not want to argue.

The next day, the same thing *happened*. The
man mountain got on the *bus*, looked at the
driver and said, 'Big John *doesn't* pay.' Then, he
went to a seat.

This *happened* for several days. After a *week*,
the driver was *beginning* to get a *little* angry.
Everybody else *paid*, so why not the big man?
So the driver went to a gym and began a course
of body-*building*. He did not want to be
frightened of Big John any more.

Two *weeks* later, the driver had strong
muscles and was *feeling* very fit. At the usual
stop, Big John got on. 'Big John *doesn't* pay,' he
said. But this time the driver was *prepared* for him.
He got up and said, 'Oh, yeah? And why *doesn't*
Big John pay?'

The man reached into his *pocket*. For a
moment, the driver was *extremely* scared.
Perhaps he had a gun? Then the man *replied*,
'Because Big John has got a *bus* pass.'

Pronunciation

1 1 a) 2 b) 3 b) 4 c) 5 b) 6 c) 7 a)

2 Ooo   oOo
  certainly   opinion
  cheeseburger   percentage
  marathon   statistics
  photograph   surprising
  tournament
  wonderful

---

5 Review 1

Grammar

1 The Key gives the parts of speech of the words as
  they are used in Units 1–4.

verbs	past tense
become	became
catch	caught
choose	chose
draw	drew
fall	fell
fancy	fancied
meet	met
pay	paid
send	sent
win	won

nouns	plural
beach	beaches
child	children
church	churches
foot	feet
mouse	mice
tooth	teeth
university	universities

adjectives	comparative
bad	worse
clever	cleverer
lucky	luckier
sad	sadder
shy	shyer
thin	thinner
ugly	uglier
wet	wetter

2
a) When did you meet your best friend?
b) Who is the tallest person in your class?
c) What is the weather like in your country?
d) How many emails do you get every day?
e) What does your teacher look like?
f) What were you wearing yesterday?

3
a) He drinks far *too* much beer.
b) How *did* your parents choose your name?
c) It *was* raining when I arrived at work.
d) There were *a* lot of people at the disco.
e) Tiger Woods is *the* greatest golfer of all time.
f) Venus Williams isn't as tall *as* Shaquille O'Neal.
g) What *are* the shops like in your home town?

4
a) was sleeping b) the most c) don't we go
d) air e) much f) few g) got
h) were driving i) saw j) looks k) don't we
l) got m) continued n) turned o) said
p) left q) looked r) they got s) enough time
t) stopped u) Can you ask

5
a) do you weigh?
b) many people at the party.
c) lot of sleep last night.
d) him two years ago.
e) you wearing yesterday?
f) more attractive than Michael.
g) as old as Inge.
h) best golfer in the world.

6 a) 5 b) 3 c) 6 d) 4 e) 2 f) 1 g) 8 h) 7

Vocabulary

1
a) F b) F c) T d) T e) T f) F g) T
h) T i) T j) F k) F l) F

2
a) out b) up c) up d) out e) down f) up
g) up h) up

3
a) noisy b) improve c) track d) funeral
e) invent f) village g) earn
Hidden words: UNIT FIVE

4
a) have b) have c) having d) get
e) make f) got g) get h) make i) make

5
a) danger b) decision c) description
d) fashion e) introduction f) luck
g) marriage h) noise i) operation j) religion
k) romance l) success

6
a) description b) choice c) operation
d) success e) danger f) marriage g) fashion
h) introduction

7
I went out on *an unusual* date with my boyfriend yesterday. He took me to a very *cheap* restaurant and I had the *worst* meal of my life. The food was *terrible* and the wine was the *least* expensive on the menu. John is *a difficult* man to be with: he's *poor, unattractive* and he can be very *boring*. When he asked me to marry him, I said...

8
appearance average height extremely
moustache intelligent friend complete
opposite overweight cheeseburger

---

6 Shop

Grammar

1
a) to b) to c) for d) for e) to f) to g) to

2
a) I told him your secret – I hope that's okay.
b) I've lent her my car.
c) Philip made her a delicious meal.
d) Why don't you get her some chocolates?
e) You need to show him/her your bus pass.
f) Give him/her the ticket.
g) I sent him/her a letter last week.

3
a) correct b) correct
c) I gave ~~for~~ my nephew a gold pen on his birthday.
d) We've brought ~~to~~ you some really good news.
e) correct f) correct
g) The shop assistant explained ~~me~~ the advantages of speed dialling.
h) She described ~~us~~ the new leopard-skin mini-skirt she had bought.

4 *Suggested answers*
a) He often drives me mad.
b) I hardly ever wear perfume.
c) She doesn't usually arrive on time.
d) I have never been to a garden centre.
e) She is rarely positive about her husband.
f) We don't often celebrate Valentine's Day.
g) I am not normally very good at choosing presents.

5
a) to stay b) spending c) surfing d) eating
e) to look f) to have g) going

Reading

1 The following sentence does not belong: 'It's often a good idea to try on one or two pairs.'

2 1 d) 2 b) 3 c) 4 c) 5 c) 6 a)

Vocabulary

1 a) evening dress b) engagement ring
c) shopping bag d) shop assistant
e) mobile phone f) price tag
g) electronic gadget

2
material	pattern
cotton	check
denim	patterned
leather	plain
silk	striped
synthetic	
woollen	

3 a) skirt b) bracelet c) earrings d) necklace
e) tie f) top g) trousers

4 a) 2 b) 7 c) 3 d) 4 e) 8 f) 1 g) 5 h) 6

Pronunciation

a) Nine hundred and twenty-five
b) Two thousand, nine hundred and forty
c) Thirteen thousand eight hundred and
    twenty-two
d) A hundred and eighteen thousand, seven
    hundred and fifty
e) Two million, seven hundred and fifty thousand,
    six hundred and five
f) Fifty million, four hundred and twenty-nine
g) Nine hundred and ninety-nine million, nine
    hundred and ninety-nine thousand, nine
    hundred and ninety-nine

7 Job

Grammar

1
infinitive	past simple	past participle
break	broke	broken
cut	cut	cut
drop	dropped	dropped
hold	held	held
know	knew	known
leave	left	left
pay	paid	paid
run	ran	run
see	saw	seen
stand	stood	stood
tell	told	told
travel	travelled*	travelled*
try	tried	tried

* *travelled* (UK English), *traveled* (US English)

2 a) has had b) Have you ever worked
c) have never been d) has ever happened
e) have hated f) Have you ever thought
g) have always wanted

3 a) this week b) yesterday c) last summer
d) this week e) over the years f) recently
g) today

4 a) ever had / have ever had
b) have always been
c) have never eaten d) started e) needed
f) had g) thought h) have always liked
i) have never made j) smelled/smelt
k) were l) often had m) was n) shouted
o) have you sold p) have not sold
q) arrested r) was s) have never been

Listening

1 c) a chef, e) a conductor

2 a) Yes b) Yes c) No d) No e) No f) Yes
g) No h) Yes i) Yes j) No k) No

3 a dishwasher

Vocabulary

1 accountant actor artist au pair banker
chef doctor farmer hairdresser midwife
nurse photographer pilot secretary teacher
vet waitress

2 a) career b) employee c) staff d) notice
e) salary f) living g) company h) application

3 a) 4 b) 5 c) 2 d) 6 e) 3 f) 1

4 a) broken b) given c) worked d) had
e) earned f) done g) happened

Writing

1 1 i) 2 n) 3 a) 4 m) 5 b) 6 c) 7 d)
8 g) 9 e) 10 k) 11 j) 12 f) 13 h) 14 l)

8 Rich

Grammar

1 a) I'm tired. I'*m* going to have an early night.
b) What about tomorrow? Are you *going* to be
    free in the evening?
c) Yes, but I'*m not* going to go out. I want to
    watch TV.
d) Are you going *to* come with me to my
    parents on Saturday?
e) No, I'm going to *see* Tony and Carla at the
    weekend.
f) Veronica, when are we going *to* get married?
g) I've already told you, Barry. We're never
    going to get married.

2 a) F b) F c) P d) P e) F f) P g) F

3 a) He's having lunch with his mum at 1 o'clock.
b) He's giving an interview at the MTV studios
    at 3 o'clock.
c) He's flying to Dublin at 6 o'clock.
d) He's attending the Music Monthly Awards
    Ceremony at 8 o'clock.

4
a) What are you going to have for lunch tomorrow?
b) What are you going to do after the lesson?
c) What are you going to do this weekend?
Students' own answers

Reading

1 Getty helps troubled Conservative Party

2 a) False b) True c) True d) False e) False f) False g) False h) False i) True j) False

3 a) party b) donated c) grateful d) addicts e) kidnapped f) mind g) fortune h) handed

Vocabulary

1 a) inherited b) bill c) rent d) profit e) save f) exchange rate g) pension h) invest i) earn

2 a) band b) single c) fans d) cancelled e) charts f) concert g) album h) gigs i) tour j) lead

3 a) 3 b) 7 c) 8 d) 5 e) 4 f) 6 g) 1 h) 2

4 a) decision b) disaster c) employment d) freedom e) performance f) popularity g) retirement h) equipment

Writing

1 a) 4 b) 7 c) 3 d) 6 e) 1 f) 8 g) 2 h) 5

Pronunciation

1
a) Who's gonna stop the rain? (Anastacia)
b) Your time is gonna come (Led Zeppelin)
c) I'm gonna be alright (Jennifer Lopez)
d) It's gonna be me (N'Sync)

2 *Wanna* is short for 'want to'.

---

9 Rules

Grammar

1 1 a) 2 b) 3 b) 4 b) 5 a) 6 a)

2
a) People could choose between the army and the navy.
b) All new soldiers had to have a medical examination.
c) You couldn't join the army if you had a physical handicap.
d) You couldn't have long hair in the army.
e) Women didn't have to do military service.
f) Foreigners did not have to register for military service.

3
a) We had to queue for two hours. / We had to wait for two hours in the queue. / We had to spend two hours waiting in the queue.
b) You should arrive at the museum early in the morning.

c) We didn't have to get a guide.
d) You shouldn't go there with young children.
e) On Wednesdays, you don't have to pay for the museum / to visit the museum.
f) We couldn't / weren't allowed to take any photos.

Listening

1 a) F b) F c) T d) T e) F

2 The following should have ticks:
b) c) d) e) g) h)

Vocabulary

1 a) sensible b) lazy c) sensitive d) optimistic e) cheerful f) insecure g) silly

2 a) Primary b) class c) Subjects d) takes e) teachers f) marks g) students

3 a) about b) for c) with d) on e) to f) of g) for h) in

4
a) 7 Physics
b) 3 Economics
c) 4 Geography
d) 6 Maths
e) 2 Chemistry
f) 1 Biology
g) 5 History

5 a) advice b) exactly c) friendly d) childhood e) embarrassing f) foreigner g) traditional

Writing

1 a) 8 b) 10 c) 7 d) 6 e) 4 f) 2 g) 9 h) 1 i) 3 j) 5

2

contracted form	full form
I haven't	I have not
I've	I have
I don't	I do not
that's	that is
I'll	I will

Pronunciation

a) could not → couldn't
b) must not → mustn't
c) does not → doesn't
d) does not → doesn't
e) does not → doesn't
f) should not → shouldn't
g) can not → can't
h) did not → didn't
i) did not → didn't
j) do not → don't
k) do not → don't

10 Review 2

Grammar

1 1 d) 2 b) 3 c) 4 a) 5 b) 6 d)

2 a) Did you ~~to~~ have to wear a uniform at school?
b) Have you been ~~go~~ to the cinema recently?
c) I couldn't ~~to~~ invite my friends to my house.
d) I don't bother ~~to~~ going into supermarkets any more.
e) I'm ~~not~~ definitely not going to forget my real friends.
f) Matt is having ~~eat~~ lunch with Madonna and Guy on Monday.
g) My husband bought ~~to~~ me a silver bracelet for my birthday.
h) She is ~~not~~ hardly ever at home in the evenings.
i) I ~~was~~ wrote an angry letter to the bank yesterday.
j) There shouldn't ~~to~~ be different rules for men and women.
k) We ~~were~~ studied this with our teacher last year.

3 *Suggested answers*
a) Last week, I lent my brother 20 euros. / Last week I lent 20 euros to my brother.
b) Unfortunately, I couldn't finish the exercise. / Unfortunately, I wasn't able to finish the exercise.
c) My mother taught me French.
d) We did not have to / need to take the car.
e) She hardly ever arrives on time.
f) What are you doing / going to do at the weekend?
g) A man in the street sold me a cheap watch.
h) I think you should / ought to call him.
i) You don't have to / need to pay for the museum after five o'clock. / You don't have to / need to pay to get into the museum after five o'clock.

4 a) than b) never/not c) told d) could
e) not f) have g) you h) her
i) must/should/can j) to k) like l) have
m) me n) tell o) living/being p) ever

Vocabulary

1 a) marathon b) runners c) give up
d) fortunately e) lift f) stadium g) winner
h) photograph i) gold medal j) found out
k) realised l) achieved m) dishonest
n) noisy o) allowed

2 a) at b) in c) about d) to e) of f) of
g) on h) for i) about j) of k) of l) for
m) over n) In o) for p) about q) of
r) up s) of t) into

3 a) confident b) famous c) friendly
d) miserable e) mysterious f) stressful
g) successful h) traditional

4 *Across*
1 stage 3 ice 5 castle 9 ring 10 album
11 wet 12 at first 14 upset 15 vote
18 bookshop 20 romantic 22 army 23 acted
24 earning 25 far 26 alive 27 thin
28 ladder 29 add 30 waste

Down
1 strawberry 2 gig 4 Chinese 6 Egypt
7 statue 8 marathon 13 sofa 16 appearance
17 disagree 19 sums 21 striped 22 advice
24 equal 27 tea

11 Smile

Grammar

1 a) Never call the waiter 'garçon' in a French café.
b) Always cross your knife and fork after a meal in Italy.
c) Never eat with your left hand in north Africa.
d) Always give a tip to New York taxi drivers.
e) Always give money to the woman sitting outside Belgian toilets.
f) Always say 'good morning' to people in English hotels at breakfast time.
g) Always take off your shoes when you go into a Japanese house.
h) Never kiss your colleagues at business meetings in China.

2 a) correct
b) I think I'll stay up ~~the evening~~ and watch the late-night movie on TV.
c) correct
d) correct
e) Why don't you sit down ~~the chair~~ and have a rest?
f) They decided to split up ~~their relationship~~ after three years together.
g) correct

3 a) Would you like to try it on?
b) you'll soon get over it.
c) I think I've thrown it away!
d) You really take after her!
e) could you turn it down, please?
f) I'm not going to take it off.
g) You must give them up immediately!

Reading

1 b) paragraph 4 c) paragraph 1
d) paragraph 2 e) paragraph 5

2 a) True b) False c) False d) False e) True
f) False g) True h) True

3 a) (the portrait of) the Mona Lisa
b) the merchant
c) (the portrait of) the Mona Lisa
d) the Louvre
e) the American expert
f) these features (the eyes and mouth)

Vocabulary

1 a) eyebrow b) eyelash c) cheek
d) moustache e) lip f) teeth

3 a) confident b) loyal c) miserable
d) mysterious e) secretive f) strong
g) warm

4 a) fill in   an application / a form / ~~a mess~~
b) get over   an illness / a problem / ~~money~~
c) give up   music lessons / smoking / ~~a coat~~
d) put on   ~~a form~~ / some music / your shoes
e) switch on   a computer / ~~smoking~~ / the TV
f) take off   your clothes / ~~a test~~ / your watch
g) turn up   ~~a job~~ / the music / the volume

5 a) down b) away c) after d) off e) up
f) with g) away

Writing

1 The first invitation is from Colonel and
Mrs Peacock. It is for their daughter's wedding.
The wedding is on April 1.

The second invitation is from David and Gavin.
It is for a New Year's Eve party.
The party is on December 31.

The third invitation is from Helen. It is inviting
Brenda to Helen's office Christmas party.
The party is on December 21.

2 1 b) 2 d) 3 a) 4 f) 5 c) 6 e)

---

12 Rebel

Grammar

1 a) He *has* a poster of Anna Kournikova on his
bedroom wall.
b) How many countries *have* nuclear weapons?
c) correct
d) correct
e) She *had* a boyfriend who worked in a circus
last year.
f) correct
g) correct
h) She *has* pink hair and a ring in her nose.

2 a) remains b) is best known c) plays
d) died e) was brought up f) went
g) was given h) was seen i) was given
j) became k) was killed

3 a) landed, was named
b) was defeated, became
c) was published, became
d) travelled, was welcomed
e) joined, were defeated
f) won, was caught
g) fought, was killed
h) was announced, did not believe

Listening and reading

1 Peaceful demonstration turns violent

2 a) done b) given c) killed d) set
e) attacked f) sent

3 a) demonstrators b) a peaceful protest
c) leaflets d) anti-police e) a fairer system
f) the law g) a group h) Our cause

Vocabulary

1 a) about b) into c) against d) in e) of
f) with g) away h) out i) at j) to

2 a) foreign ministers b) student fees
c) fur coats d) bottle banks
e) public transport f) plastic bags
g) nuclear weapons h) protest marches

3 a) organisation b) fascination c) separation
d) legalisation e) decision f) exhibition
g) reduction h) decorations

4

1	2	3	4	5	6	7	8
g	a	c	b	f	h	d	e

Writing

1 a) small number b) Most c) several
d) large number e) none f) a few
g) nobody h) majority

---

13 Dance

Grammar

1 a) since b) for c) for d) since e) since f)
for g) since h) for
Students' own answers

2 a) gone b) been c) been d) gone e) been
f) gone g) been h) gone

3 a) has been a fashion model since
b) has been famous since
c) have been married for
d) has been in New York since
e) have known him for
f) has he had

4 a) have been b) have been building
c) have been saving d) have been dancing
e) has been f) has had

Reading

1 Billy Elliot — Jamie Bell
Billy's father — Gary Lewis
Billy's brother — Jamie Draven
Billy's grandmother — Jean Heywood
The dance teacher — Julie Walters
Michael — Stuart Wells

2 a) 7 b) 1 c) 3 d) 2 e) 6 f) 5 g) 4

3 a) ✓ b) ✓ c) ✗ d) ✓ e) ✓ f) ✗
g) ✓ h) ✗ i) ✗ j) ✓

4 a) best-known b) follow in his footsteps
c) ridiculous d) express yourself
e) a key moment f) for all tastes

Vocabulary

1 a) flamenco b) waltz c) samba
d) rock 'n' roll e) reggae f) pop

2 a) nightlife b) clubs c) dance floors
d) room e) live f) DJ g) House h) stage

3 a) at b) on c) on d) at e) at f) on
g) on h) at

4 a) pretty b) guy c) reckon d) knackered
e) winding him up f) laid-back

5 a) about b) to c) for d) for e) on f) of
g) with

Writing

1 1 c) 2 a) 3 b)

2 a) because of b) because c) because
d) because of e) because f) because of

---

14 Call

Grammar

1 1 a) 2 c) 3 c) 4 b) 5 a)

2 a) Do you think he will return my call?
b) Can you remember what time the meeting is?
c) Could you tell me how much a beer costs?
d) Do you know if he passed on the message?
e) Do you know what 'worried sick' means?
f) Could you tell me what you think of my outfit?
g) Can you remember who you spoke to?

3 a) Can you remember where I put my car keys?
b) Do you know how much this costs in dollars?
c) Could you tell me where the theatre is?
d) Do you think it is against the law?
e) Do you know if she is married?

Listening

1 a) Conversation 2
b) Conversation 1
c) Conversation 3

2 a) Is …. there, please? 1
b) Who's calling? 1
c) I'd like to speak to … 2
d) Could I speak to ….? 3
e) Sorry, she's not in at the moment. 1
f) Thank you for calling. 2
g) I'll put you through. 3
h) Can you tell her I called, please? 1
i) Please hold. 2
j) You've got the wrong extension. 3
k) Can I take a message? 1
l) No one is available to take your call. 3

Vocabulary

1 a) operator b) dialled c) extension
d) message e) voicemail f) call g) mobile
h) line

2 a) told b) said c) said d) asked e) told
f) said g) asked h) told i) said

3 a) on b) at c) on d) at e) in f) on g) in
h) in i) at j) on

4 a) hang b) pick c) put d) give e) come
f) get g) run h) pass

5

1	2	3	4	5	6	7	8
b	g	c	a	f	h	e	d

Writing

1 1 Mr Sharma from Credit Bank called. Call him back: 020 768 9004.

2 Richard called – he's cancelled tennis this evening. Next week okay.

3 Mary from AWOL Travel says your tickets for Bangkok are ready.

2 *Suggested answers*
Petra called about your advertisement for a babysitter. Call back after 6 o'clock – 0474 355899.

Brenda called – meeting at the office with someone from the Tax department 8 o'clock tomorrow morning. Very important.

15 Review

Grammar

1

verbs	past participle
agree	agreed
carry	carried
commit	committed
enjoy	enjoyed
hide	hidden
hold	held
kidnap	kidnapped
rob	robbed
run	run
throw	thrown

nouns	plural
factory	factories
illness	illnesses
knife	knives
luxury	luxuries
roof	roofs
toe	toes
wife	wives

adjectives	superlative
bossy	bossiest
deep	deepest
easy	easiest
good	best
rude	rudest
silly	silliest
untidy	untidiest
wide	widest

2
a) Do you like James Bond films?
b) Are you thinking of going out tonight?
c) Have you been abroad this year?
d) How long have you been living here?
e) Have you been to the cinema recently?
f) Would you like me to help you?

3
a) A Che poster *was* pinned on his wall when he was a student.
b) How long *have* you been studying English?
c) I *have* been a DJ for two years.
d) I was wondering *if* you could lend me your car.
e) Is it okay *if* I bring my friend?
f) Rosie *is/was* looking for a new place to live.
g) She *was* kidnapped by a revolutionary group.

4
a) have you been b) for c) told d) to help
e) looked f) buying g) allowed h) thought
i) to go j) tell k) thought of him l) put it on
m) was asked n) have come o) he is
p) replied q) Join r) at s) have been waiting
t) for

5
a) Don't be late.'
b) pardoned by President Clinton in 2001.
c) took the photo of Che.
d) been to the cinema for a month.
e) been a DJ for two years.
f) like me to call you later?
g) you could take a message.

6 a) 8 b) 1 c) 7 d) 3 e) 6 f) 4 g) 2 h) 5

Vocabulary

1 a) T b) F c) T d) T e) F f) F g) T
h) F i) T j) T k) T l) F m) F

2 a) over b) up c) up d) through e) up
f) off g) out h) out

3 a) enjoyed b) volume c) inherit d) starred
e) illness f) organic g) naughty
Hidden word: REVISION

4 a) got b) got c) have d) had e) make
f) had g) get h) made i) make

5 a) cruelty b) demonstration c) difficulty
d) education e) explanation f) explosion
g) information h) legalisation i) mystery
j) pollution k) science l) tradition

6 a) confidence b) education c) information
d) demonstration e) legalisation f) difficulty
g) explanation h) cruelty

7 It was a *cold*, *wet* day and we were driving *fast* down a *narrow* street in the town. My husband is a *careless* driver and he *never* stops at red lights. Suddenly, another car drove into the *front* of our Mercedes. *Unfortunately*, my husband is a very *violent* man, and he's always very *rude*. He got out of the car...

8 usual worried nervously finally carefully absolutely wrong replied scream people concert

16 Lifestyle

Grammar

1
a) you *will* be relaxed and positive about life.
b) you *will* feel younger and more healthy.
c) your energy levels *will* be much higher.
d) relationships with your friends *will* be happier.
e) your general fitness *will* improve.
f) you *will* change the way you think about food.
g) your friends *will* think you look wonderful.

2 *Suggested answers*
a) He won't be relaxed and positive about life.
b) He probably won't feel younger and more healthy.
c) His energy levels definitely won't be much higher.
d) Relationships with his friends definitely won't be happier.
e) His general fitness probably won't improve.
f) He won't change the way he thinks about food.
g) His friends definitely won't think he looks wonderful.

3 a) comes b) will say c) is d) will think
e) loses f) eats g) asks

4 a) isn't, will take
b) will have, doesn't speak
c) get, will call
d) are, 'll look
e) 'll go, want
f) isn't, 'll find
g) 'll tell, get

Reading

1 Genetically modified fast food *paragraph C*
The danger to the environment *paragraph B*
What is added to your fast food? *paragraph A*

2 a) 2 b) 6 c) 1 d) 3 e) 4 f) 5

3 a) ingredients b) health c) Research
d) packaging e) environment f) modified

Vocabulary

1 a) a healthy life b) your fitness c) fit
d) a walk e) weight f) yoga g) stress
h) holiday

2 a) spinach b) grape c) trout d) prawn
e) pepper f) garlic g) carrot h) aubergine
i) cucumber j) lettuce k) chicken l) sausage

3 b) 3 c) 6 d) 8 e) 2 f) 7 g) 1 h) 4

4 a) calorie b) junk c) recipe d) snack
e) starving f) vitamins

5 a) not my cup of tea b) packed in like sardines
c) a piece of cake d) full of beans

Pronunciation

a) break b) peach c) friend d) receive
e) abroad f) youth g) mountain

---

17 Animal

Grammar

1 a) who b) who c) that d) that e) who
f) who g) that h) who

2 a) that b) that c) — d) that e) — f) that
g) that h) —

3 a) would you try b) came c) invited
d) would you do e) asked f) would you feel
g) would you give
Students' own answers

Listening

1 The order is: d), b), c), a).

2 1 b) 2 a) 3 a) 4 b)

Vocabulary

1 ant bear camel cat cheetah cow deer
dog dolphin elephant fish giraffe hamster
horse iguana kangaroo mosquito parrot
pig rat reptile snake spider tortoise

2 a) dog b) spider c) snake d) kangaroo
e) parrot f) giraffe g) cheetah h) horse

3 a) wait b) deer c) write d) bear e) weight

4 a) bored b) afraid c) keen d) worried
e) tired f) approve g) fascinated h) think

---

18 Weird

Grammar

1 1 a) 2 b) 3 b) 4 a) 5 a) 6 a)

2 a) had seen b) had missed c) had had
d) hadn't studied e) had been engaged

3 a) had arrived b) spoke c) discovered
d) had been e) was f) was g) discovered
h) had got married i) had died j) heard

4 a) heard b) realised c) had died
d) looked e) asked f) had lost g) took
h) had gone i) had died j) discovered

Reading

1 1 d) 2 f) 3 a) 4 e) 5 c) 6 b)

2

1	2	3	4	5	6	7	8
e	c	a	f	g	h	b	d

Vocabulary

1 a) many b) old c) well d) often e) long
f) far g) much
Students' own answers

2 a) take b) take c) make d) have
e) have f) take g) make h) make

3 a) jealous b) embarrassed c) in a bad mood
d) proud e) sad f) on top of the world
g) excited h) frightened

4 a) flight b) investigation c) explanations
d) permission e) description f) development
g) confidence

Pronunciation

a) Yes, I've seen about a *thousand*.
b) The first crop circle was seen in *1980*.
c) We found it in the *morning*.
d) No, we think it was made by *aliens*.
e) Yes, it's more than a *kilometre wide*!
f) No, I've *never* seen one like *this*.

19 Wheels

Grammar

1
a) The roads used to be quiet and safe.
b) no change
c) I used to be very proud of my bike.
d) I used to clean it every day.
e) My best friend used to be a boy called Tom.
f) no change   g) no change   h) no change

2
a) If I were you, I'd choose a good language school. / I'd choose a good language school if I were you.
b) You could look for a job there.
c) Why don't you stay with an English family?
d) If I were you, I'd go in the winter. / I'd go in the winter if I were you.

3 *Suggested answers*
a) The roads used to be less busy.
b) There used to be fewer people.
c) There didn't use to be advertisements.
d) There didn't use to be any tourists.
e) There didn't use to be black taxis.

Listening

1
Speaker 1 b)
Speaker 2 c)
Speaker 3 a)

2

	Speaker 1	Speaker 2	Speaker 3
What colour is it?	✗	white	red
What special features has it got?	✓ beds kitchen table loo television	✓ black windows shiny wheels cocktail bar DVD	✓ car stereo
How fast does it go?	✗	✗	✓ 400 km/hour
Where would you like to go in your car?	✓ Ireland	✓ Hollywood	✓ Monte Carlo
Who would you take with you?	✓ grand-children	✓ friends	✓ Jennifer Lopez

Vocabulary

1
a) steering, gear   b) belts, seats
c) engine, bonnet   d) wheel, boot
e) windscreen wipers

2
a) public transport   b) air conditioning
c) hair style   d) traffic jam   e) fast food
f) health care   g) summer holiday
h) driving licence

3
a) dangerously   b) partly   c) heavily
d) casually   e) closely   f) intelligently
g) specially   h) abroad

4
a) powerful   b) spacious   c) electric
d) polluted   e) aggressive   f) considerate
g) angry   h) safe   i) wise

Writing

1 to give advice about travelling in England

2

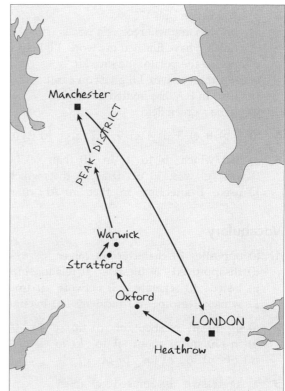

3 I suggest that you ...   (And) you could ... why don't you ...

Pronunciation

1 The second speaker sounds more positive. She uses a higher tone of voice.

20 Review 4

Grammar

1 1 d) 2 c) 3 b) 4 b) 5 a) 6 d)

2
a) We will have a break when we ~~will~~ finish this exercise.
b) That's the man I told you about ~~him~~.
c) I've got a friend who ~~she~~ got married last week.
d) They ~~were~~ used to live in Madrid.
e) If you read more books, your English ~~it~~ would improve.
f) I would ~~to~~ see a doctor if I were you.
g) I hope I will ~~to~~ find a good job soon.
h) When he had finished breakfast, he ~~had~~ left for work.
i) She used to have ~~wearing~~ long, blond hair.
j) Why don't you speak to someone who ~~he~~ understands the problem?

3
a) you revise Unit 17?'
b) finishes first will receive a prize.
c) finish / have finished my work, I'll help you.
d) peeled the potato, she sliced it.
e) our train arrives, I'll give you a call.
f) lives in L.A. has invited me to visit.
g) to be a green field.

4 a) 6 b) 8 c) 5 d) 4 e) 9 f) 7 g) 1 h) 2 i) 3

5 a) that/which b) to c) in d) than e) he
f) was g) was h) of i) as j) that/which
k) used l) after/for m) that n) At o) was

Vocabulary

1
a) opposite b) character c) career
d) disapproved e) lifestyle f) relationship
g) lasted h) separated i) network j) trouble
k) while l) escape m) incidents n) eventually

2
a) of b) at c) about/of d) up e) in f) as
g) in h) In i) about j) To k) to l) of
m) of n) to o) for p) of q) on

3
a) aggressive b) amused c) angry
d) believable e) jealous f) spacious
g) surprising

4 Maggie was always *unlucky* with men and one day she tried a computer dating agency. She was looking for a *weak* personality because she was quite *shy* herself. A week later, the agency found a man. They said he had *little* in common with her and they were sure their first date would be a *failure*.

Before going out, Maggie *forgot* to brush her teeth and put on her new perfume. She smelled *awful*! Feeling quite *nervous*, she arrived at the restaurant, which was almost *full*. Then, she saw him, sitting at a table with a *silly* expression on his face. It was definitely him. It was her *previous* husband!

5 *Across*
1 windscreen wiper 6 jam 8 prawn 9 ate
10 pet 11 abroad 14 aliens 15 studio
16 causes 18 carrot 19 recipe 21 fur
22 pig 23 cheap 24 add 25 air conditioning

Down
2 I haven't a clue 3 snake 4 experts 5 dead
7 lawyers 12 road 13 all of a sudden
15 strange 17 soup 19 rage 20 igloo